The Red Grange Story

The Red Grange Story

An Autobiography

As Told to Ira Morton

Foreword by Robert C. Zuppke

New Introduction and Afterword
by Ira Morton

University of Illinois Press
Urbana and Chicago

Illini Books edition, 1993
© 1953, 1981 by Margaret Grange and Ira Morton
Reprinted by arrangement with the copyright owners.
Introduction and afterword © 1993 by Ira Morton
Manufactured in the United States of America
P   5   4   3   2   1

This book is printed on acid-free paper.

Library of Congress Cataloging-in-Publication Data
Grange, Red, 1903–1991
    The Red Grange story : an autobiography / as told to Ira Morton ;
foreword by Robert C. Zuppke ; new introd. and afterword by Ira
Morton. — Illini books ed.
        p.   cm.
    Reprint. Previously published : New York : Putnam, 1953.
    ISBN 0-252-06329-5 (alk. paper)
    1. Grange, Red, 1903–1991.   2. Football players—United States—
Biography.   I. Morton, Ira.   II. Title.
GV939.G7A3   1993
796.332′092—dc20
    [B]   93-11212
                                                                        CIP

It is with a deep sense of gratitude that I dedicate this book to the University of Illinois. Everything good that happened to me in my life stems from the roots I planted there as a youth.

—Harold "Red" Grange

Contents

Illustrations follow page 88

Introduction

Following World War I, Americans were eager to forget the tension, perils, and tragedy of the war years. They were looking for peacetime heroes who could provide a diversion, and they found them on the playing fields of sports arenas, where athletic skills rather than guns were the weapons used to defeat an adversary. Those combatants who shone above the competition in a given sport were lifted out of the pack and placed upon a special altar reserved for sports idols. The process was helped along by sportswriters of the stature of Damon Runyon and Grantland Rice, who rhapsodized about the unparalleled feats of these athletes, dubbed them with colorful nicknames, and wrapped them in myth. This was the "Golden Age of Sports."

Two names emerge as the central figures of this unique period in Americana: Babe Ruth and Red Grange. This book is the story of one of them, just as he told it.

Harold "Red" Grange began his legendary football career at Wheaton High School, where he crossed the goal line seventy-five times and became the most highly publicized high school athlete in the state of Illinois. At the University of Illinois he amassed a total of 3,637 yards by running, 643 yards by passing, and scored thirty-one touchdowns. His collegiate statistics are remarkable considering he averaged forty-five minutes of playing time on both offense and defense and appeared in only twenty-one games. When Grange played in 1923–24–25, freshmen were not permitted to play on the varsity and the season was limited to eight games. Today most freshmen are eligible for four years of competition and the regular season has been expanded to eleven games. Imagine the extent of his total offensive numbers had Illinois's three-time All-American been given the opportunity to compete in twenty more college games.

In three varsity seasons Grange ran for over 100 yards eleven times, exceeded 200 yards on three occasions, and reached the 300-yard mark twice. And this was accomplished against some of the strongest opponents in the nation, teams like Nebraska, Iowa, Ohio State, Minnesota, the University of Chicago (when it was the Big Ten Conference Champion coached by the venerable Amos Alonzo Stagg), and the University of Pennsylvania (then regarded as the best team in the East). However, it was in the Illinois-Michigan game of October 18, 1924, that Grange ascended to an even higher level of play and became an American sports legend.

Illinois met its arch-rival from Ann Arbor on a warm, sunny day at Urbana-Champaign before a sellout crowd of 67,000. Students, faculty, and alumni turned out in record numbers to celebrate the dedication of Memorial Stadium (the playing field was later named for Robert Zuppke) and see their campus hero in action. Avid football fans from all over the state poured into the college town by car and rail in the hope of witnessing more Red Grange heroics. None of those in attendance would be disappointed.

Grange took the opening kickoff on the Illinois five-yard line and headed upfield like a cheetah chasing prey. Within seconds he crossed Michigan's goal line, untouched. The stadium erupted in the first of a series of thunderous, nearly deafening ovations. Before twelve minutes of the first quarter had elapsed, Grange scored three more times on runs of 67, 56, and 45 yards. In the third quarter he ran for a fifth tally, and in the final period he passed for a sixth. At game's end, the junior halfback had accounted for 402 yards on the ground and 78 in the air as Illinois trounced Michigan 39-14.

Red Grange's performance in that Illinois-Michigan game is regarded as the greatest one-man show in the annals of college football. Grantland Rice covered the event and was inspired to describe in poetry what he saw. It was through his feelings, spirit, and words that the Illini superstar would forever be "The Galloping Ghost." Sixty-seven years later, in the fall of 1991, *Sports Illustrated* remembered the event in its special classic issue, titled "A Celebration of Yesterday's Heroes." Of all those featured, the magazine chose to put Grange's picture on the front cover and devoted a full page to his historic feat against the Wolverines.

Up until the end of Grange's senior season at Illinois, the thought of turning pro never entered his mind. This was understandable, for the National Football League was then perceived as a playground for macho characters with mediocre talent. The press gave the NFL very little coverage, with the result that fan support was minimal and the average pay for players was twenty-five dollars a game. Unlike most of today's college athletes who dream of playing in the NFL, Grange went to the university for only one reason: to get a good education so he could qualify for a decent job after graduation. If he participated in intercollegiate athletics, it would only be for fun and the opportunity it provided to earn a modicum of recognition among his peers on campus. This modest youthful goal was to change dramatically when he met a man named Charlie Pyle.

Pyle's only claim to fame at the time was that he owned a couple of Champaign movie theaters. However, he was ambitious, persistent, cunning, and unbelievably persuasive. Recognizing the magnetism "The Galloping Ghost" engendered all across the land, he came up with a bold, imaginative plan: he would lure Illinois' superstar to sign a contract to play professional football and then peddle his services to the Chicago Bears. Pyle was convinced Grange could earn a million dollars as a pro if the Bears' top brass could be talked into a 50-50 split of the gate receipts.

Pyle first approached Grange with his wild scheme toward the end of the 1925 season, but the Illinois senior was uninterested and suspicious that the theater owner was either a flake or represented the Capone mob. However, Pyle relentlessly pursued Grange and finally managed to get his signature on a contract immediately after his last college game, against Ohio State. The possibility of making a million dollars was much too tempting for a poor college boy to pass up.

Just prior to the signing, Pyle met in Chicago with

George Halas and George Sternamen, co-owners of the Bears, and after lengthy, grueling negotiations lasting into the night, he got them to agree to his stiff terms. Five days after the game with the Buckeyes, on November 26, 1925, "The Galloping Ghost" showed up at Wrigley Field in a Bears uniform for his professional debut against the Chicago Cardinals.

In past seasons the Bears' management was thrilled if the team attracted a crowd of 5,000, but on that Thanksgiving Day Wrigley Field was filled to capacity. Thousands more were lined up around the stadium at game time hoping to get in. This sudden avalanche of fan interest was directly attributable to the extensive newspaper coverage of Grange's decision to cast his lot with the pros. (In those days sporting events depended entirely upon newspapers for publicity as radio was in its infancy and television was yet to be born.)

Following the Cardinal game, which ended in a 0-0 tie, the Bears went on to play eighteen games from coast to coast over the short span of sixty-six days. Battered and bruised, Grange was forced to sit out two games due to injuries, but he still managed to average thirty minutes of playing time in the remaining contests. When the extended season ended on January 31, 1926, "The Galloping Ghost" had crossed the goal line seventeen times, thus partially satisfying the more than 400,000 fans who passed through the turnstiles to catch a glimpse of their hero in action. The important thing was that professional football got the exposure it desperately needed, fans were impressed with the quality of play, and the NFL finally came of age.

Red Grange made $125,000 in his first year as a pro and another $85,000 in endorsements and a movie deal. It may not seem like much compared to the millons earned by today's superstars, but in 1925–26 it was considered a fortune. Those were the days when you could buy a new car for $400, eat a full-course meal at a good restaurant for less than a buck, get a haircut for fifteen cents, and buy a decent suit for around ten dollars. Grange was now rich, and he had Charlie Pyle to thank for it. Pyle thus became America's first super sports agent and was annointed by the press with the nickname "Cash 'n' Carry."

Red Grange played professional football for eight more seasons before retiring in 1935 at age thirty-two. Due to a serious knee injury that kept him out of action during the entire 1928 season and forever stripped him of his speed and mobility as a runner, he never made the million dollars Pyle had promised him. However, he still performed well enough on both offense and defense in his comeback attempt to ultimately be selected as a charter member of the Professional Football Hall of Fame. From a historical perspective, Grange managed to gain everlasting recognition as the man who single-handedly provided the catalyst that put the NFL in business as a major sports attraction.

As a young boy growing up in Chicago, I was very familiar with the Grange name. In my mind Red Grange was to football what Babe Ruth was to baseball. I never saw Grange play, but I clearly remember going to the neighborhood theater on Saturday afternoons to watch him elude sinister pursuers in a thrilling thirteen-episode serial called "The Galloping Ghost." Later, while a journalism student at the University of Illinois, I became inbued with the Grange mystique and could almost feel his presence when attending games at Memorial Stadium.

Some years later, in the summer of 1950, while working as a columnist for a Chicago newspaper, I suddenly came up with the idea of writing Grange's life story. A mutual friend arranged an introduction, and I met Red for the first time in his downtown office. He greeted me in a warm, friendly manner and listened carefully to my proposal that we do his life story as an "as told to" autobiography. Then he asked some questions about my schooling and journalistic credentials. No more than an hour had elapsed when he said, "You're the first to come to me with this idea. I like it and I like your enthusiasm. Besides, you're a fellow Illini. Let's do it." This newly established professional relationship was to blossom into a close friendship that lasted until Red's passing some forty-one years later.

It took nearly three years to complete the book — and that included a six-month hiatus while Red recovered from a heart attack. We met every two weeks at his northside apartment. I often brought along my tape recorder, and I would set it on the kitchen table, hand Red the microphone, and start asking questions. After each working session, which usually lasted about two hours, Margaret Grange would serve refreshments and the three of us would sit around and visit on a personal level.

Red's power of recall amazed me. He remembered

minute details of almost all the major and minor events of his life. However, I did not trust everything to his memory. Countless hours were spent at the Chicago Public Library turning the crank on the microfilm machine searching for quotes, feature stories, news items, and eyewitness accounts of Red's college and professional games. It was an education to read the works of the brilliant sportswriters who chronicled "The Golden Age of Sports"—not only Runyon and Rice but Ford Frick, Westbrook Pegler, Warren Brown, and Walter Eckersall.

I believe it is worth mentioning that in all the print research that was done for this book and in numerous personal interviews with Red's contemporaries, I never read or heard any negative comments or allegations about his personal conduct on or off the field. He was looked upon as the ideal sports role model, and that image was never to change.

During the course of writing this book, and in countless conversations in the years following its initial publication in 1953, I do not recall hearing Red use foul language or even imply a racial or ethnic slur. To him everyone was an individual whose strengths and flaws came from within rather than from any outside factors of race or ethnicity. Although competitive to the core and tough physically, there was nothing macho in his personality. He was humble, kind, gentle, and surprisingly sentimental.

The extent of Red's modesty was unbelievable. Coach Bob Zuppke saw fit to mention this outstanding character trait in the foreword he wrote for this book. I learned the depth of Red's humility firsthand when I wrote to Ray Elliot in 1979 suggesting that a statue of Red Grange be erected outside the main entrance to Zuppke Field. Elliot, Zuppke's successor as coach and at the time director of athletics at Illinois, responded swiftly: "I think it is a remarkable idea and I will bring it up at the next board meeting and see if we can get some action." But when I called Red at home in Florida to tell him what we were up to, he wanted no part of it. "I appreciate what you tried to do, Ira," he told me, "but this is embarrassing. There are so many great football players who played for Illinois, it wouldn't be fair to single me out. Please call Ray and tell him to forget about this statue thing. If he asks why, tell him what I said." I had no choice but to carry out his wishes, and the idea was dropped.

Red Grange has been called the greatest all-around football player of his generation, perhaps of all time. His legendary feats on the gridiron grow more wondrous with every passing year. What impressed me most about the man, however, was that his basic character, personality, and ideals remained unchanged despite all the fame and adulation.

Ira Morton
Phoenix, Arizona

Foreword

I have watched an endless number of football players down through the years, but never have I seen anyone quite the equal of Harold "Red" Grange. He came nearer to being the perfect football player than anyone I have ever known. What made him the football immortal that he is? I think I can sum it up in these words: exceptional football abilities, courage, willingness to learn and, above all, his modesty.

It has often been said that all Grange could do is run. The fact is, he could punt, pass, block and tackle with the best of them. But when he did run he was something to behold. He was the smoothest performer who ever carried a pigskin. He ran with rhythm, every movement of his body having meaning and direction. On the gridiron, Red Grange was a football stylist, a symphony of motion.

Red was not only as fast as they make them once he got into the open, but an unusually fast starter. Since football is a series of fast starts and pickups, the ability to get away fast is of immense value. As soon as I recognized this talent in him I dropped all and any part of my previous "T" formations and used what I called "The Grange Formation." In this formation I placed Grange five and a half yards behind the line of scrimmage so as to allow his blockers a fraction of a second more time to take their men out, thus preventing him from running into his own interference.

At the end of Red's junior year in 1924, Grantland Rice, the famed sports writer who has a poet's way with words, described his great running ability thus: "Grange runs as (Paavo) Nurmi runs and (Jack) Dempsey moves, with almost no effort, as a shadow flits and drifts and darts. There is no gathering of muscle for an extra lunge. There is only the effortless, ghostlike weave and glide upon effortless legs with a body that can detach itself from the hips—with a change of pace that can come to a dead stop and pick up instant speed, so perfect is the co-ordination of brain and sinew."

One of Grange's greatest physical assets besides his wonderful pair of legs, was his uncanny peripheral vision, which enabled him to see to the sides as well as straight ahead. This made it possible for him to get a panoramic view of the playing field at an instant glance, and probably explains why he had such a great sense of timing and could dodge and twist, both to his left and right, and pick up his interference as effortlessly as he did.

Grange was game to the core. His aim was always to win, always to give his very best. For him there was no such thing as mediocrity or taking it easy. As a result he took an enormous amount of punishment, but did so without ever flinching or complaining.

To have a boy like Red Grange play for you was a coach's dream. He wanted more than anything else to be a great football player and welcomed any advice or suggestions that would help him along in that direction. I never had to tell him anything twice. He learned fast not only because he was smart, but because he had the proper attitude. He never got to be so good that he couldn't learn any more. Grange was determined from the very beginning to continue growing in stature not only as a player but as a man, and his later life has borne that out.

For Red, his conscientiousness and determination went hand in hand with an innate modesty which proved to be the lifesaver of his team's morale. He caught the imagination of the public like no football player before him. Because of the tremendous acclaim he acquired, many of the boys who played with him did not receive the credit due them. Jealousy on the part of his teammates could easily have developed, thereby ruining the team and his own individual career. It was Grange's tact bred by his modesty which caused his teammates to remain consistently strong and loyal. He was always quick to give credit to those who helped him and always voiced the opinion that his success was due largely to the efforts of the ten other men on the field.

The qualities of character which contributed toward making Red Grange the greatest name in football are those same qualities which have made him the outstanding citizen that he is long after his playing days are over. He continues to be a credit to football, his university and former associates. He has proven himself to be a durable character on and off the field. I know of no finer example of true American sportsmanship than the "Galloping Ghost" of Illinois.

ROBERT C. ZUPPKE
Champaign, Illinois

The Red Grange Story

1

The Early Days

AT THE TURN of the century, Forksville, Pennsylvania, was a small town of some two hundred inhabitants with most of its men working in the nearby lumber camps. It was situated in a picturesque setting of giant hemlock trees, clear, cool creeks, green grass and majestic mountains. Forksville was, however, a rustic, isolated community over fifteen miles away from the nearest railroad and farther yet from the closest towns of Williamsport and Wilkes-Barre. The town had one ancient-looking hotel, a general store that sold everything from plows to needles, and a schoolhouse with all eight grades in one room.

It was in this hamlet that I was born on June 13, 1903, the third child of Sadie and Lyle Grange. My father, the foreman of three lumber camps owned by the late Pennsylvania State Senator Charles W. Sones, was Scotch-Irish, and my mother of English extraction. I had two older sisters named Norma and Mildred and a brother, Garland, born two years after me.

I have very few memories of my early days in Forksville, since my family moved from there when I was five years old. I vaguely remember such things as coasting down the steep, snow-coated hills on a sled in the wintertime, the spring floods, the two covered bridges that spanned the two creeks in the town and the fishing I did in those creeks. I also have a faint recollection of the gypsy bands that came to Forksville every summer and how frightened I was that they'd steal my dog Jack. I was crazy about that dog and played with him by the hour. My favorite pastime was to back Jack in the corner of the fence and watch him dodge, fake and squirm his way out of my grasp. He was unquestionably the greatest open-field runner I ever saw, and I learned things from him I never forgot.

There are two things that stand out in my memory about the Forksville days. They are the annual county fair and the lumber camps where my father worked. I recall how interested I was in the baseball games and track meets that were held at the fair and how I tried to emulate the older boys who participated in those events. One day after watching one of the track meets I went home and attempted to pole vault with a homemade pole I fashioned from a branch of a tree. The pole snapped when I applied pressure and part of it ran into my side, breaking two ribs. As far as I know, this was my first athletic injury.

It was always a thrill to visit my father at one of the lumber camps. Whenever I'd come around, one of the teamsters would put me up on a horse and let me ride while they were skidding the logs. When I wasn't on a horse I would stand and watch for hours the thunderous spectacle of the logs sliding down the

4

mountainside and the way the men worked feverishly to break the log jams in Loyalsock Creek.

My father was a man for a kid to brag about. Besides being a great woodsman, he weighed more than two hundred pounds, stood a shade over six feet tall and was so fast and quick on his feet for a big man that he could lick anybody in the countryside. That's how he got to be a lumber-camp foreman. Lumberjacks are generally pretty rough, tough characters and the only way a man could rate as the boss-man over such a crew was to be tougher than any man working for him.

There was only one other lumberjack who ever seriously threatened my dad's position as the town Goliath. This man was bigger than my father and fancied himself the town bully. The two men had a showdown one day, battling for six hours in the woods until the bully, battered to a pulp, finally dropped into a state of unconsciousness. After this no man ever dared stand up to my father again.

My mother died when I was five. Several months afterward, my father moved the family to Wheaton, Illinois, where his four brothers and one sister lived. When we got to Wheaton, Dad rented a small home and went into the house-moving business with Uncle Sumner. Before long he decided it wasn't a good plan to raise girls without a mother, so he sent my sisters back to Pennsylvania to live with my mother's folks. At first Aunt Bertha took care of Garland and me during part of the day while Dad worked, but later a housekeeper was hired when my aunt left Wheaton to become Dean of Women at Houghton College in upstate New York.

A few years passed and my father, Garland and I, moved in with Uncle Luther, who was a bachelor. By the time I entered eighth grade we changed our address again, with Dad and Garland sharing a small apartment above a store while I moved in with Uncle Ernest on his farm. I lived with Uncle Ernest for about a year—a year I'll never forget.

The following was a typical day on Uncle Ernest's farm. Rising at five A.M., I'd head straight for the horse and cow barns and put in about an hour's work feeding hay and oats to five horses and milking four cows before sitting down at the breakfast table. After breakfast I had to water the horses, then hitch them up to the wagon and drive into town to deliver the milk to the local dairy. Returning to the farm, I'd get on my bicycle and pedal two miles to school. At night, just before retiring, it was my job to clean out the barns, get the hay down for the next morning, feed the horses and milk the cows again. Needless to say, I earned my keep—and then some. After a year of this my father was convinced Uncle Ernest was working me too hard and took me back to live with him.

I found Wheaton to be quite different from Forksville. With its nearly four thousand residents, Wheaton was a bustling metropolis by comparison. But it didn't have the beautiful, mountainous terrain of Forksville. Nevertheless the air was still fresh and

6

clear and there was lots of room for kids to play. Most important, it offered a more civilized way of life. At first I missed Forksville terribly, but as the years rolled on I realized more and more the advantages of growing up in Wheaton. Had the family remained in Forksville, I might have ended up as another Huckleberry Finn.

The school system of Wheaton was quite an improvement over Forksville, but that meant very little to me during my elementary-school days. I hated school just like any other kid and was resigned to it simply as a duty. The more important part of living came after school when I was able to play football, basketball and baseball with my pals.

We used to play football in a vacant lot near the edge of town. None of us had uniforms, but improvised by cutting off the pant legs of our oldest trousers and added padding where needed most. The lot we played on was convex in shape, with fifty yards of the field on one side of a hill and fifty yards on the other. On a kickoff the ball would sail up and over the top of the hill, seemingly coming from nowhere. By the time a player tucked the pigskin under his arm and started up the field behind his interference, the opposition would suddenly swarm over the top like "The Charge of the Light Brigade." It was enough to scare the daylights out of a kid.

On the football field I tried my darnedest to be like my two special heroes, All-Americans Bart Macomber and Potsy Clark of Illinois. This ambition was completely frustrated at the time since I insisted on playing with the older kids who made me look pretty sad by comparison. I took quite a beating, too. Once I got kicked in the spine and couldn't sit down for two weeks. I was always getting the flesh around my eyes cut open and frequently had to have stitches taken. Many times I got so discouraged I wanted to give up playing football in favor of shooting marbles or playing tops. It was my father who encouraged me to continue. He said it would make a man of me.

Besides the bruises I received from football, I got my share of bloody noses and blackened eyes from fighting. I usually got whipped in these bouts by one of the older boys. My dad, running true to form, offered no sympathy in this connection. I remember well how he impressed upon me that it was more important to fight fairly than to win a fight. This object lesson in sportsmanship stayed with me all my life.

Wheaton had no YMCA or gymnasium for the kids in those days. When the basketball season rolled around we converted neighborly Lawrence Plummer's barn loft with a hoop and used it for practice. A church basketball league and a Boy Scout league were formed for the kids in the town and we got to play most of our games in the Wheaton College gym. I kept active as usual, playing on teams in both leagues. Those of us who played took our basketball seriously—with the result we had some pretty fair teams. Looking back, I'm glad I played a lot of basketball as a kid, for it's a wonderful game to develop one's legs for football.

In the summer, besides playing a great deal of

8

baseball, I spent many hours with my pals touring the surrounding towns on our bicycles. Usually we'd pedal until near exhaustion. Riding a bicycle was also great for the legs.

The summer also brought the inevitable church picnic with its races and various games of skill. The first time I entered a race for youngsters under eight I was awarded a baseball for winning. At those picnics I won at least one race every year I participated. I had quite an incentive since my dad gave me a quarter every time I won. Speaking of running, I am convinced it is impossible to coach a youngster to run faster than his natural gait. Speed is something you're born with—it can't be taught. I was lucky enough to have it.

Like most kids, I tried my hand at caddying because it seemed like a nice, clean way to earn some spending money. However, after the first day of staggering through seventy-two holes, I decided it wasn't the kind of work I cared to do too often.

When I was eight years old, my athletic career ended almost before it began. A doctor, called in to treat me for an ordinary cold, said I had developed a heart murmur and that I no longer should be allowed to engage in any strenuous exercise. Needless to say, my father was crushed by the news. I was pretty unhappy, too, but just like a boy didn't realize the supposed seriousness of my condition. After a few weeks I began to sneak out after school to play in the neighborhood games. This went on for several months without my father being the wiser.

Then one day I suffered a back injury from playing football, and when I got home made a determined but unsuccessful attempt to conceal the pain from my dad. He made me confess how it happened, and when he found out, instead of being angry, was completely sympathetic. He decided then and there that since athletics meant so much to me he wasn't going to interfere any more, despite the doctor's orders.

In making this decision without consulting further with a physician, Dad took a big gamble. As it turned out I suffered no ill effects, and if I did actually have a heart ailment as a child, it disappeared. The only explanation I can give of this strange incident is that the heart murmur diagnosed by the doctor was functional instead of organic, and as such was merely a temporary condition.

When I entered Wheaton High School I had my first thorough physical examination since I was eight. Although Dad and I had almost forgotten about the heart scare of nearly six years back, we nevertheless breathed a sigh of relief when they pronounced me to be in top physical condition. And I was. Although a bit long legged, I had a rugged physique for a youngster. The vigorous outdoor life I led in Forksville and Wheaton helped build up the stamina and endurance that I needed in the years that followed.

2

Winning Sixteen Letters in High School

I ENTERED Wheaton High School in the fall of 1918. At the time I was living with my father and brother in a five-room apartment over one of the stores in the downtown district. Dad, who was a one-man police force in Wheaton, barely made enough to support the three of us. We were so poor all I did during my high-school years was attend classes, study and participate in athletics. I never went out on dates with girls, because I didn't have any money or a decent suit of clothes to wear. The little I earned during the summers working on an ice truck was needed for the bare necessities of life.

Our high school was housed in a rickety, old three-story red-brick building with a high tower on top. J. B. "Prof" Russell, the superintendent of Wheaton's public schools, had his office in that tower. All the teachers at Wheaton High, including Miss Ella Gregg the principal, were women—with the exception of Roy Puckey, the manual training teacher. Since Puckey had some knowledge of sports, he was forced into doubling up as the coach of all the school's athletic teams.

I went out for football a few days after enrolling in high school. Reporting for practice, Puckey asked me what position I played. I inquired in return what positions were open and was informed all the boys except the right end were back from last year's squad. Without hesitation I informed Puckey I was a right end. Starting off at that position, I played there my entire freshman season.

Having just turned fifteen and weighing a mere 138 pounds, I took quite a beating playing high-school football as a freshman. I clearly remember how nervous and self-conscious I was in my first game. It seemed like everyone was watching me and I got to the point where I wished I hadn't gone out for football. Wheaton won that first contest in spite of me, but succeeded in winning only one other the rest of the season.

As a freshman I was a good tackler, could run and get down fast under kicks. Being tall I was able to reach up high for passes, although much to my disappointment no one ever threw any at me during the games. The one and only time I carried the ball that first year, I made a touchdown. It was in the last contest of the season when I grabbed the ball on a kick-off and scampered nearly seventy yards to the goal. After the run my teammates pounded me on the back and made some flattering remarks about my belonging in the backfield. Taking them seriously, I made a bid for a backfield berth the next fall. I told Bill Castleman, the school's new manual training teacher and football coach, that I was really a halfback and played end the year before merely because the team needed someone for the position. Castleman let me have a whirl at it and I became the regular left halfback. I played at that position my sophomore, junior and senior years.

Our football field was located in an apple orchard a mile and a half from school. It was no easy task walking that distance every night after a strenuous practice session. The freshman members of the team lined the playing field and cleared away the stray apples on Saturday mornings before the games. Regardless of how careful we were to remove the fruit from the ground, we'd always miss a few. I got juice squirted in my eye dozens of times falling on those apples. Wheaton High finally built a football stadium in 1926 and incidentally, named it Grange Field.

We usually had a crowd of around two hundred at our football games. There were no seats, so the people stood around the sidelines and walked up and down with the plays. Admission was free, but a hat was passed around and the school collected from twenty-five to fifty cents per person. That, along with the limited budget Wheaton had for athletics, helped pay for football and most of our other sports.

The high school furnished us with all the necessary football equipment except shoes and helmets. I had a hard time trying to scrape up enough money for those two items. In the end I could afford only a second-hand helmet from a boy who graduated the year before, which made it necessary for me to borrow shoes from the other players on the team when they weren't in the game. During my freshman year I never wore a pair of football shoes that fit me.

After finishing my first football campaign, I went out for basketball. Wheaton had one of its finest teams a few years before, but the season immediately prior to my enrollment Elmer Hoffman, Beans DeWolf, Hip Conley, Ode Voigt and Larry Brooks, all the members of that outstanding team, had graduated together leaving the race for positions wide open. Under those conditions I was able to make the squad my first year along with my close pal Lawrence Plummer, the boy in whose barn I used to play during my grammar-school days. With all the practicing we did in the hayloft we got to be pretty good shots. I was elected captain of the basketball squad my first season and kept that honor through my sophomore year.

Our initial game of the 1918-19 season was against the Wheaton alumni. Their team was made up entirely of the five players I mentioned as comprising the greatest team in Wheaton's history. When we beat them handily the townsfolk began to sit up and take notice of us.

My first two years at Wheaton I played center and the last two years operated at the forward position. Beginning with my freshman season, I managed to win many all-sectional honors and have always felt that basketball was my best game even though I never participated in the sport at Illinois.

In the spring I went out for track. I ran the 100 and 220, broad jump and high jump, and both the

14

low and high hurdles. Beginning as a freshman I usually entered all six events at a meet and on many occasions won all of them. My best time in the 100 was 10 seconds and the farthest I ever broad jumped was close to twenty-three feet. My high-jump limit was about six feet.

Wheaton High School didn't have a track of its own so we'd jog about three miles every day to Wheaton College's Lawson Field. We also used the college gym for basketball practice three times a week and played our games there on Saturday nights.

I was captain of the track team my sophomore, junior and senior years. The last two years I represented Wheaton in the state meet for class B schools which was for schools with enrollment under five hundred. At those meets I won the 100, 220 and broad jump in alternate years. The winter of my senior year a Little Seven Conference was organized. It was made up of Geneva, Naperville, St. Charles, Batavia, Dundee, Sycamore and Wheaton. At our first annual track competition in St. Charles I won six events and made several marks that were to stand for almost twenty years.

The sport I liked best in high school was baseball. I went out for the team the same time I went out for track and played baseball whenever we didn't have a meet. With baseball not being considered as important as football, basketball and track at the time, we didn't even have a regular ball field to play on. We had to set up our own diamonds on the various vacant lots around Wheaton. The baseball squad as well as all other teams at the school used the same locker room, which was located in the basement of the school building. With only one shower, it often took us more than an hour to get out of there.

Throwing and batting right-handed, I played all the positions including pitcher and catcher—although my ambition was to be a first baseman. I wanted to be like Vic Saier, the great first sacker of the Chicago Cubs. I had a strong throwing arm and could hit pretty well, too. However, when I played baseball down at Illinois, I couldn't bat worth a lick when the coach changed my batting stance.

When I said earlier all I did while attending high school was go to school, study and participate in athletics, I neglected to mention one other activity. I did all the cooking at home and, if I have to say so myself, was a darn good chef. My brother Garland did the shopping and we took turns washing and wiping the dishes. We also did the house cleaning ourselves since Dad was generally too busy to help with any of these chores. The only relaxation my father had was to attend Wheaton's basketball and football games. Although he never participated in either of these sports as a boy, he grew to be a tremendous fan and to my knowledge never missed a game while I was in high school. He considered attending these contests part of his official duties. It would have been an easy matter to rob a bank while a game was going on.

As a sophomore on the football team I scored ninety-nine points, making fifteen touchdowns and kicking nine extra points. My greatest asset that first season as a halfback was, besides my ability to run fast, my use of the stiff arm. By building up great strength in my arm working on the ice truck, I was able to push away many would-be tacklers.

During my junior year I worked hard to learn how to dodge and throw my hips away from a tackler as he was about to hit me. The results amazed me, for that year I improved to the point where I scored 255 points with thirty-six touchdowns and thirty-nine conversions. In one game I scored eight times and made all the extra points. We won by such lopsided scores as 83-0 and 41-13, and wound up undefeated in our DuPage County League made up of seven teams in Chicago's western suburbs.

Of the seven teams in the conference, our toughest rival was Naperville. We always beat them in football but in basketball it was generally pretty even. A few years before I entered high school, a big slug fest took place after a football game between Wheaton and Naperville, and during the excitement someone clobbered DuPage county's Sheriff Kuhn over the head with a monkey wrench. The sheriff was laid up for some time and relations between the two schools were nearly severed as a result of the incident.

One of the most pleasant recollections of my Wheaton High School days concerns the Charles Dollinger family. The Dollingers were the parents of Charles, Jr., a close buddy and teammate of mine on the basketball and football teams, and for three years, whenever I wasn't cooking at home, I ate my meals at their house. Mrs. Dollinger was a kindly, gentle woman who gave me the mothering a boy of my age needed. Her husband, known affectionately as "Doc" to all the residents of the town, owned the corner drugstore. After a game he would serve free sodas and sundaes to all the members of the teams. "Doc" had one of the first Buicks in Wheaton and would drive many of the players home from the games and take a gang of us out on Sundays to a cottage they had at Powers Lake, Wisconsin. They were a most generous family. To this day I still have the scrapbooks which Mrs. Dollinger kept for me when I was at Illinois.

My grades in school were always pretty good, but to me were just a means to an end. I studied mostly because I had to stay eligible. I remember the time in my second year when I almost lost that eligibility through cheating in Latin, which was my poorest subject. I had the English translation written over the Latin and because I neglected to space the words properly, didn't turn the pages with the others. It didn't take the teacher long to recognize what I was up to. She told me to stay after class and I was scared stiff I'd be reported and ruled off the basketball team that year. I was greatly relieved when she let me off easy by merely warning me never to be guilty of such conduct again. I heeded the warning from then on.

In my last year of football competition at Wheaton I crossed the goal line 23 times and kicked 34 points after touchdown, which added up to 172 points. All told, in three years of high-school competition I made 75 touchdowns, including the one of my freshman year, and booted 82 conversions for a grand total of 532 points.

Wheaton won every game but one my senior year. We lost 39-0 when we went up to Toledo to play the powerful Scott High School eleven. In that game I got kicked in the head early in the first quarter and was carried unconscious from the field. I didn't come to for almost forty-eight hours and then could hardly talk for days afterward. It was the only time I was ever seriously hurt playing high-school football. However, I frequently had stitches taken around my eyes, because of my bad habit of tackling low which caused me to get cut by the players' heels.

Before our loss to Scott High we licked two strong teams by big scores including a 21-0 victory over Austin High School, the runner-up for the High School Championship of Chicago that fall. After the sad experience at Toledo, we won the remainder of our season's games and against Downers Grove I scored six touchdowns as we trounced them 63-14 for the League Championship. That game was like a track meet. We were all so exhausted from making long runs, we considered the possibility of pulling the tackles back to carry the ball for a while.

Toward the end of my senior year at Wheaton I was officially contacted by a college for the first time during my high-school career. Carl Johnson, one of Michigan's all-time track greats, came down to Wheaton with a few other Wolverine alumni to sell me on the idea of going to their school. Since athletic scholarships were unknown at that time they offered no financial assistance. I was very flattered at their interest in me, but could not see my way clear to meet the expenses involved in attending an out-of-state institution.

I finally wound up at the University of Illinois for three reasons. First, because it was the least expensive school I could go to as a resident of the State of Illinois. Second, my neighbor, George Dawson, played on the Illinois football team and made me Illinois conscious by constantly talking up his alma mater. The third and most important reason had to do with the strong impression Coach Bob Zuppke made when I went down to Champaign in my senior year for the state high-school interscholastic track competition. Zup was very warm and friendly and I remember him saying, "If you come down here to school I believe you'll stand a good chance of making our football team." Those few words of encouragement from one of football's greatest figures meant more to me at that time than it is possible to express.

3

"The Wheaton Iceman"

MOST ATHLETES are generally branded early in their playing days with a nickname which is supposed to best capture the imagination of the fans. I had two such names. Besides the "Galloping Ghost," I was called "The Wheaton Iceman." It was only natural I be given more than one nickname since I had two separate careers. I was a football player in the fall and an iceman in the summer.

I don't remember who hung "The Wheaton Iceman" title on me, but it sure caught on in a big way with the sports writers of the day. Although it turned out to be a swell publicity break, I honestly never intended it as such. I got into the ice business simply because I needed to earn money and it was my first chance to land a full-time job. I kept at it for eight summers upon making the discovery that delivering ice was an excellent way to keep in shape. Reporting for football in the fall after a summer on the ice truck, I would be tough as nails and at least four weeks ahead of the other boys in conditioning. My iceman's duties made my arms, shoulders and legs strong and developed my wind. It was, in effect, my own private brand of "spring training."

21

I began my eight-year hitch as "The Wheaton Iceman" the week after I was graduated from grammar school. It started one day when Luke Thompson, the owner-operator of an ice truck, thought he'd have a bit of fun with some of the neighborhood kids. He promised one dollar to the boy who could lift a seventy-five-pound cake of ice on his shoulder. Just as he figured, none of the boys could lift the ice above their knees. Thanks to some experience I had with ice tongs while working for several years after school as a helper on an ice wagon I succeeded in getting the load up on my shoulder and Thompson was forced to make good his sporting offer. Actually, I had very little occasion to use a pair of ice tongs before, since my job on the ice wagon consisted mostly of watching the horse while the driver made deliveries.

Impressed with my being the only kid able to lift the ice to shoulder height and already having made an investment in me, Thompson invited me to work with him on his ice truck for the entire summer. The job sometimes required working fourteen hours a day, from five in the morning to seven at night, six days a week, but I jumped at the opportunity as the weekly wage of $37.50 seemed like more money than I ever dreamed it was possible to earn.

An iceman's job is a rough, tough, bruising business. I well remember all the agonizing moments when I jabbed myself with the ice pick, got the ice tongs stuck in my skin and dropped huge cakes of ice on my hands, feet and toes. None of these mishaps were serious, however, except one which almost cost me my athletic career.

This near-tragic accident was the result of a careless habit I had of jumping on the running board of the ice truck while it moved down the street between deliveries. One morning early in July, between my sophomore and junior years in high school, the handle alongside the cab of the truck, which I usually grabbed for support when I jumped on the running board, broke off in my hand. I tumbled to the street and under the truck which was loaded with three tons of ice. Before the vehicle could be brought to a stop, the back wheel ran over the meaty part of my left leg slightly above the knee.

I was momentarily stunned as Herman Otto, who worked the route with me, nervously lifted me into the truck and drove off to a doctor's office. When I got over the initial shock I became almost panic-stricken at the thought that I might never play ball again. When the doctor first looked at me he feared the knee was crushed and amputation of my leg would be necessary. Luckily, further examination revealed the wheel missed within an inch of involving the knee joint and there was no need for such drastic action.

Although my leg had been saved, I was given no better than a fifty-fifty chance for complete recovery. I worried constantly about this while confined to bed for almost a month with my leg uncomfortably hanging in a sling. My family and friends were equally concerned and did everything they could to cheer me up. There was nothing for me to do but lie on my back and wait for nature to take its course.

Fate was kind, for in a matter of two or three weeks after I got out of bed I was walking again with little ill effect. By fall I was well enough to report for football. Strangely enough, although I don't think the injury ever hampered my ability to run, my left leg has remained partly numb to this day.

Luke Thompson felt particularly bad about the accident and did everything he could to help. He met all my doctor bills, besides continuing to pay my weekly salary. I didn't resume my chores on the ice truck that summer, but was back on the job the following year still convinced that being an iceman had more advantages than disadvantages.

An iceman's job can be hazardous in other ways as well. In this connection I recall the lady who threatened that her husband would lick me for tracking up her kitchen floor. Even though I apologized repeatedly, she refused to be forgiving. The very next time I delivered ice to her home she pointed a condemning finger in my direction and ordered her spouse to "teach that young punk some manners." If he had been a big brute I might have been in trouble, but as luck would have it he was more worried about the spot he was in than I was. This was due to the plain fact that I outweighed him by at least thirty-five pounds. His wife was the one who could have really done me some harm since she was bigger, and certainly more ferocious, than either of us.

As the husband moved toward me he winked in an

obviously friendly manner and I immediately sensed his problem. It was clear he was only interested in making an impression in front of his wife. I went along with his little game by letting him shake me and tell me off in especially strong terms while I just stood still and acted like a boy afraid. About an hour after I left he caught up with me in his automobile and thanked me profusely for "making me look so brave in front of the old lady." As a further token of gratitude he slipped five dollars in my pocket.

There was only one other time I missed work on the ice truck in eight summers and that was one afternoon several weeks before the injury to my leg. On that particular morning I worked from five A. M. to noon, then took the rest of the day off in order to participate in the Wheaton community track meet. My boss didn't appreciate the idea, but agreed to let me go when I pleaded, "Just this once." Although somewhat tired when arriving at the meet, I was so excited to be there, I managed to win the 100- and 220-yard sprints, high jump, broad jump, high and low hurdles —and I still have the loving cup to prove it. Since that was the only track meet the town of Wheaton ever held during the summers I worked as an iceman, I kept my promise to Thompson and never willfully neglected my job again.

As I said, my working day averaged about twelve hours. Sometimes on Saturdays I worked as many as fourteen hours. Regardless of how many hours I put in, after dinner I used to throw a baseball or football around with my brother Garland and a close pal named Lyman DeWolf until dark. By nine P.M. I was usually in bed. On Saturday nights I wanted to go out on dates or be with the fellas just like any other boy my age, but I was generally so tired after a hard week's work that all I wanted to do was sleep. Sunday was the one day I enjoyed complete rest and relaxation. It consisted of sleeping almost to noon, attending a baseball game in the afternoon and then taking a train into Chicago to see an early evening movie and vaudeville show.

This was the kind of life I led during the summers while I went to high school and college. While it's true it may seem like a pretty dull existence, there was a definite purpose to it. As a youngster I wanted more than anything else to be a great athlete, and I realized early that it meant giving up many of the things other kids didn't have to give up to achieve that ambition. Like anything else in life, success in athletics cannot be attained unless one is willing to sacrifice for it.

An iceman discovers very quickly that some housewives can be quite different in the kitchen than in the parlor. Most of my customers were easy to do business with, but to be sure I had my share of troublesome ones. For example, there was the woman who challenged the accuracy of the weight of a one-hundred-pound cake of ice she ordered. Having read in a newspaper how the weight of ice could be determined from its measurements, she got out the tape measure when I delivered the ice to her door one day and, after making the necessary calculations, decided the ice was considerably below the one-hundred-pound mark. I insisted she was wrong, that if anything it weighed more than one hundred pounds, but she refused to believe me. If I expected to collect for the order, I'd have to prove its weight.

I had little choice but to lug the now slowly melting ice down two flights of stairs to the ice truck, half a block away. While my skeptical customer stared intently, I placed the ice on the scale and much to her embarrassment it tipped the beam at 105 pounds. Before carrying the load up to her apartment again, I made her agree to pay the difference for the extra poundage.

I also remember an experience with a lady who thought she invented a sure scheme to get free ice. On occasion she accepted and paid for her order just like anybody else, but most of the time would greet me at the door with, "Oh, I'm terribly sorry young man. I don't need any ice today. Guess I just plum forgot to take my ice card down." Since she lived at the end of an unpaved, dead-end street that was impassable for motor vehicles, I'd leave the ice a few yards from her front gate rather than cart it back to the truck parked a block away. This went on for the better part of a summer until one day I accidentally spotted the old witch retrieving the ice after she thought I had left the vicinity. The next time she attempted to dupe me I promptly dumped the ice on her front lawn and chopped it up in a million pieces.

I was tagged as "The Wheaton Iceman" the summer following my sophomore year at Illinois. It was the result of a publicity stunt that had me posing with a cake of ice on my shoulder with a couple of shapely beauties from the "Artists and Models" show running at the Apollo Theater in Chicago. The picture that was taken subsequently appeared in newspapers all over the country. It was the first time any mention had been made in the press of my summertime job, and the idea of a college football star doubling as a hardworking iceman seemed to catch the public's fancy.

When I returned to Wheaton in the summer of 1926, after completing my first year of pro football and then making a movie in Hollywood, I took my old job back on Luke Thompson's ice truck. A lot of folks thought I was out of my mind. They figured it was a comedown for a guy who had made as much money as I had that year. But I didn't look at it that way. I was convinced, as always, that working on the ice truck was the best possible way to stay in condition. And, after all, that was of the utmost importance since I was still a football player and not a banker.

There was one slight change, however, in my working habits after I got into the chips. I can truthfully say I performed all my iceman's chores as conscientiously as before, it was just that I drove to and from work in my $5,500 Lincoln Phaeton instead of hitching a ride. Thompson used to rib me about that, saying, "Red, please don't park that thing in front of my place. It kinda confuses me as to who's working for who."

When I went to college, athletes were not given any financial assistance. Regardless of how great a boy's athletic talents were, he had to pay his way through school just like any other student. I didn't receive a dime in the nearly three and one half years I spent at Illinois. I depended almost entirely upon the money I earned as "The Wheaton Iceman" to pay my expenses. As it turned out, working on the ice truck was one of the greatest things that ever happened to me in my development as a football player.

It is an accepted fact the most important parts of a football player are his legs. Keeping those legs in shape represents the biggest single responsibility of a boy interested in playing football. While working on a road gang, laboring in the coal mines or steel mills is good for general muscle development, it contributes nothing toward keeping a player's legs in condition. One stands still when working at those jobs and doesn't use his legs. Delivering ice, which required my walking miles every day up and down stairs, kept me in all-around fine trim and provided the best possible off-season training for my legs. And I never became afflicted with rheumatism as many predicted I would from being exposed to the cold and dampness of the ice.

The important thing for a player to remember is that football isn't a game that can be played just three months in the fall. In order to excel in the sport, one must constantly work at keeping his body and, especially, his legs strong the other nine months of the year. I have known many potentially great football players who never attained their full capabilities because they had to spend the entire football season getting back into condition after a lazy summer. I was offered all kinds of soft jobs during the school vacation periods, but always turned them down in favor of sweating it out on the ice truck. I was a fanatic on the subject of conditioning.

It is practically an impossibility for a football player to set up his own training program. Almost superhuman will power is required to whip yourself into playing condition after even a slight lay-off. The trick is to get the kind of job during the off season that will, by its demands, keep one fit without actually realizing it. My job on Luke Thompson's ice truck filled the bill to a *T*.

4

First All-American Honors

WHEN I ENROLLED in the University of Illinois
in the fall of 1922, I pledged the Zeta Psi fraternity
which, incidentally, turned out to be the only luxury
I was to enjoy during my stay at the university. George
Dawson, the Wheaton boy who originally talked me
into going to Illinois, was a member of that fraternity.
Arriving on the campus with the battered, second-
hand trunk my father bought for me, I must have
looked more like a refugee from Siberia than a university student.

A few days after I moved into the fraternity house,
the upperclassmen informed the pledges of the school
activities in which they were to participate. Since I
felt my best sports in high school were basketball and
track, I planned to go out for those two sports at college, but the Zeta Psi's had other plans for me. They
figured that since I also had a pretty good record in
football at Wheaton High, it would be much more
desirable, prestige-wise for the fraternity, if I were to
concentrate on football. I argued that at 166 pounds
I was too light for college football, but being a mere
pledge my objections were of no consequence.

The first day I reported for practice, I took a look

at some one hundred and fifty beefy candidates for the freshman team and became all the more convinced I didn't belong. Without even putting on a uniform, I went back to the fraternity house and complained. "What chance have I got against all those big guys?" My protests met only with a deaf ear and the threat of a paddling. Under the circumstances, I decided it would be wise to at least give it a try. The next day I went out for the freshman team in earnest, but still felt deep inside I didn't have a chance in the world to make the grade. However, when I took a longer look around I discovered much to my surprise that although most of the aspirants were much bigger than I, they couldn't run as fast nor handle a football as well. I began to get a little more confidence.

Before a week had passed, the squad was culled down to sixty. It was hard for me to believe I was not only still around, but put on the first-string team. The backfield in that number-one line-up included Ralph "Moon" Baker at quarterback, Earl Britton at fullback, Paul Cook at right halfback and myself at left half. No sooner had Burt Ingwersen, the frosh coach, picked his starters, than we found ourselves pitted against the varsity in a regulation game. Although the varsity nosed us out 21-19, I scored two touchdowns in that game, one on the return of a sixty-yard punt. From that day on I was "made" as a freshman. At the end of the season I was to be named captain of the frosh eleven.

After that first encounter with the varsity, we

scrimmaged them regularly twice a week. Ingwersen used to key us up for those games just as if they were for the Conference Championship, and most of the time we beat the Illinois team handily. We outweighed them almost ten pounds per man in the line and had a faster backfield. Coach Bob Zuppke became so enthused with our potentialities he spent more time with us than he did with the varsity. It is an accepted fact the 1922 freshman team was one of the strongest Illinois has ever had. Two members of that squad besides myself subsequently became All-Americans. Ralph "Moon" Baker gained his honors at Northwestern where he transferred after his freshman year. Tackle Frank Wickhorst, who also left Illinois at the end of his first year, went on to become an All-American at Annapolis. Although Earl Britton failed to win All-American recognition at Illinois, he nevertheless is regarded by many to be one of the greatest blocking backs and kickers ever developed in the Western Conference.

An extremely hot rivalry existed between the varsity and the freshmen in 1922. I remember one particular incident involving Roy "Windy" Miller, the regular varsity guard, whose constant heckling of the freshmen players led to a minor revolt against him. During one of the regular varsity-frosh battles, we cooked up a play whereby the entire freshman team hurled itself en masse at "Windy." The play was so successful Miller ended up with a broken nose, a bruised body and a more than slightly dented ego.

However, Coach Zuppke chewed us out plenty for that as Miller was needed for an important conference game the next Saturday.

When I was issued my frosh football equipment neither the shoes nor the uniform fit me properly. Before I could wangle another pair of shoes, I had developed corns and blisters on my feet. The number on the back of my ill-fitting jersey happened to be 77. It was just dished out to me, I never asked for it. I got to thinking it was pretty lucky and asked to keep it permanently when I returned in my sophomore year.

Much credit for the excellent performance of Illinois' 1922 freshman squad must be given to Coach Burt Ingwersen. He taught us many of the important fundamentals of the game—fundamentals that most of us missed in high school. Only twenty-six at the time, having played his last game as an Illinois lineman some five years before, Ingwersen was young enough to understand our problems yet mature enough to cope with them.

After the freshman football season, I went out for intramural track. Teaming up with Larry Wright, a high jumper from the Zeta Psi house, we won the intramural cup for our fraternity. I managed to win first place in six events in the final meet. In the spring of 1923 I reported for spring football practice with the varsity, which consisted of about nine weeks of hard, serious work under Bob Zuppke's tutelage. That spring I came to realize more than ever before that no mat-

34

ter what your abilities or hopes may be, there is no short cut to being a good athlete.

I'll never forget what George Dawson said to me after I rounded out my first year at the university. He sat me down one night and cautioned: "Red, I'm convinced you have what it takes to become a great football player, but don't ever let it go to your head. Never get to the point where you think you're better than the next guy, because if you do, you'll never go on to realize your full capabilities." Dawson's words made an indelible impression on me.

I reported for fall practice my sophomore year in good shape, having worked hard all summer on the ice truck. Naturally I hoped to make the first-string varsity, but Zuppke gave no indication the previous spring whom he would select as his regulars. When the season opened, however, I happily found myself in the starting line-up.

Our first game of the 1923 season, on Saturday, October 6th, was on old Illinois Field against the Nebraska Cornhuskers. Anyone who has ever played football knows what goes through a player's mind in his first game. I was shaky and nervous and when I looked at the opposing players they looked like they weighed about three hundred pounds per man. At the end of the first quarter Zup called me aside and said, "You're leaning, Red, and giving away the plays." It was hard for me to believe this since I was so excited I didn't know myself where the plays were going. In spite of all my fears I had a pretty good day. I scored all of Illinois' touchdowns as we beat Nebraska 24-7. My first tally was made on a wide thirty-five-yard run around right end and I got away for a sixty-yard sprint for the second one in the next period. Fullback Earl Britton kicked all goals after touchdown and booted a twenty-seven-yard field goal in the second quarter. Walter Eckersall, the one-time Chicago football great turned sports writer, predicted in his write-up of the game for the Chicago *Tribune:* "It was a spectacular piece of work, the sort expected of a player with the speed of the former Wheaton star who has all the earmarks of developing into a wonderful player."

After meeting the Cornhuskers, we took on Butler and again won, this time by a 21-7 score. In that contest I accounted for two more touchdowns while our right guard, "Mush" Crawford, chalked up the other. Britton, already beginning to show his phenomenal ability as a kicker, booted all three goals. With two straight wins under our belts we traveled to Iowa City the following week to open our conference schedule against Iowa.

Iowa was a great football team and I wondered if we could do as well against them as we did against Nebraska and Butler. It was a fierce battle all the way, but we finally won the game 9-6 in the closing minutes of the last period. I slid over for the touchdown after Britton connected with me for four out of five passes. When the game was only four minutes old, Britton put Illinois ahead 3-0 with a sensational field goal from the fifty-three-yard line. I held the ball for Britton and I can honestly say it gave me my greatest thrill in football. There was such power to that kick it shot out almost on a line as it cleared the uprights.

Several hours before the Iowa battle Coach Zuppke called his team together for an important chalk talk in the ballroom of the Jefferson Hotel. Counting noses, he discovered everyone present but Earl Britton. When no one could tell where Britton was, Zuppke sent Captain Jim McMillen, our left tackle, out to look for him. McMillen searched everywhere in the hotel until finally one of the elevator operators told him he took a big fellow fitting Britton's description up to the roof. Following the tip, the Illinois captain found his burly, six-foot-three, 240-pound fullback on the roof making airplanes out of hotel stationery. Since it was Iowa's Homecoming, a big parade was going on in the street below, so Britton scribbled, with school-boy enthusiasm, "To hell with Iowa" on the wings of his airplanes and sailed them out into the crowd. This was typical of Britton's carefree attitude which made him a wonderful guy to have around. He always seemed to come up with something to take the pressure off the team when it was most needed. In the case of the paper airplanes, for example, the players got such a laugh when they heard about it, it helped them relax and lose any tension they might have had before the game.

The next Saturday we played Northwestern at Cubs Park and won by a 29-0 margin. My contribution in that game was a ninety-yard run in the first quarter when, with Northwestern threatening, I intercepted a wildcat pass on our own ten-yard line. Northwestern seemed to become so demoralized after that run, they appeared to lose their fight. Britton, incidentally, kicked one point after touchdown and a field goal from the thirty-five-yard line.

At this stage of the season, newspaper writers began referring to me as the Galloping Ghost, the name which was to stick with me for the rest of my life.

After beating Northwestern, we played our toughest game of the year against the formidable University of Chicago eleven. The game was played to a near-capacity crowd of 61,000 people in Champaign on November 3rd, 1923, at the opening of Illinois' Memorial Stadium. Near the end of the first quarter, I intercepted a Chicago pass on our fifteen-yard line and ran it back sixty-two yards to their twenty-three-yard line, but we failed to score from there. About halfway through the third period I made a touchdown after a march that Illinois started from our thirty-seven-yard line. In that drive Right Halfback Wally McIlwain's line smashes gained steady yardage and I made fifty-three yards in seven attempts. Two plays before that touchdown, I had crossed the goal line from the twenty-yard mark but was ruled out of bounds on the seven. Britton added the extra point and when neither team scored in the fourth quarter, we topped Chicago 7-0. Altogether I gained 173 yards that day in seventeen plays.

After the Chicago battle we whipped Wisconsin on our home grounds 10-0. I made the only touchdown early in the first quarter after a series of end runs of fourteen, twenty-five and twenty-six yards. Britton kicked the extra point and a thirty-three-yard field goal. In the second period I was nailed hard by a tackle and just about made it to half time. I stayed out of the game the entire second half. A week later Illinois used its subs to take Mississippi A. and M., 27-0. Neither our Quarterback Harry Hall nor I played, but Earl Britton and Wally McIlwain saw action for a little more than a quarter. Britton was in long enough to add two more kicks after touchdown to his already impressive total.

We wound up the 1923 season on November 24th at Columbus by defeating the Buckeyes from Ohio State 9-0. For three quarters we battled to a standstill as Ohio State played inspired ball. They gained considerable yardage and threatened often with a formidable passing attack. Their key players, Quarterback Hoge Workman and Right Halfback Ollie Klee, played brilliantly both on offense and defense. Illinois' offense, on the other hand, couldn't get rolling. It seemed as though the Buckeyes were laying for me, for every time I carried the ball they swarmed over me like a hoard of buzzards. Britton's movements were also especially well guarded. In the final period, however, the tide swiftly turned. Britton kicked a thirty-two-yard field goal and several minutes later I broke away for thirty-four yards and a touchdown. Britton narrowly missed the point after touchdown, but we had accounted for all the points needed for victory.

By subduing Minnesota 10-0 the same day we defeated Ohio State, Michigan finished the season with four conference wins and no defeats to share the Big

Ten Championship with Illinois. Our record was five wins and no losses. The previous year Michigan earned a tie for the title with Iowa.

At the end of my sophomore season I led the Big Ten scorers with twelve touchdowns and seventy-two points. Halfback Earl Martineau of Minnesota was runner-up with seven touchdowns and one kick after touchdown for forty-three points. Earl Britton scored twenty-six points that season with eleven kicks after touchdown and five field goals. Between Britton and myself we accounted for ninety-eight of our team's 136 points.

Captain Jim McMillen, Illinois' fine tackle, was listed on practically every All-Western eleven in 1923, as was Frank Rokusek, our left end. For my work that year, Walter Camp, the father of intercollegiate football, named me as the left halfback on his All-American Team. Camp commented:

> Red Grange of Illinois is not only a line smasher of great power, but also a sterling open-field runner and has been the great factor in the offense of Illinois through the middlewest conference. He is classed as the most dangerous man in that section and probably the country over, when all kinds of running must be considered.

After the football season I decided to rest up for a few months and concentrate more on my studies. But when spring rolled around I couldn't resist the urge to go out for baseball. Although my hitting left much to be desired, I became Illinois' regular center fielder. My main assets as a ballplayer were speed, a strong arm and the ability to field well. In my junior year, baseball coach Carl Lundgren had me alternating between the pitching mound and the outfield, and I earned a 1-1 record as a pitcher. At the end of my second season of college baseball I was offered a big-league tryout with the Boston Braves, but I turned it down because I didn't feel in my own heart I was good enough to make the grade as a big-leaguer. I certainly had no ambition to make a career in the minor leagues. Besides, there was still another year of college football competition left for me and I didn't want to pass that up.

5

"Illinois vs. the Conference"

MOST FOOTBALL FANS are probably aware of the existence of football scouts. They know the function of these scouts is to observe and study the opposition so the teams they work for can, as a result of their findings and recommendations, properly prepare a defense and attack. And it is accepted as a fact that many football games have been won because of a scout's astute observations.

To fully appreciate the enormous contribution a scout can make to a team's success one must see what goes into an actual scouting report. This is well-nigh impossible, however, for a scouting report with its diagrams, charts and detailed evaluation of strategy is about as confidential as Army Intelligence and FBI documents.

Even players rarely get an opportunity to see a scouting report, as the results of these reports are usually interpreted to them by their coaches. The first time I saw a scout's handiwork was many years after I left Illinois when Tucker Smith, then head trainer at Ohio State, privately presented me with his school's original scouting report on the 1923 Illinois eleven.

Being an old friend from the days when he was assistant trainer at Illinois under Matt Bullock, he took the report from the files himself thinking I might like to have it. I might add there was no breach of ethics involved, because at the time he gave it to me all the players written up in the report had long since graduated.

Titled "Illinois vs. the Conference," the Ohio State report is a completely objective appraisal of Illinois' great team of 1923. Its contents are, I believe, worthy of inclusion in a book such as this. For the benefit of the vast majority of football followers who are not usually concerned with the highly technical aspects of the game, I have selected for publication only that material in the report which might be of interest.

Beginning with an analysis of our offensive strength, the report read: "The Illinois offense this year is built around "Red" Grange and Earl Britton. Grange carries the ball practically 75 per cent of the time on short and wide end runs, off tackle, and cutbacks. His end running attacks are successful due to two things: one, a wonderful superman who uses all the tricks of a good halfback's stock in trade; and two, some extremely effective interference and blocking. It seems as though the Illinois players sense that certain feeling when blocking for Grange. They block with much more vim and vigor for him than any other Illinois back.

"If the Illinois end running attack of Grange is stopped, they will resort to their desperation passes from Britton to Grange like they did in the Iowa

43

game. And there again, this man Grange becomes a nightmare. Against Iowa, Grange cut across back of the line of the defensive team and took passes on the dead run high over his head. Down the field under long passes and on short passes over the line he consistently went up in the air and caught the ball although surrounded by three or four Hawkeyes.

"It is recommended that if we can stop Illinois' end running and they then resort to this Britton to Grange combination, we spot a floating pass defender who will cover Grange wherever he goes.

"Britton is a long and accurate passer, but his chief offensive strength lies in his wonderful and powerful toe. He is an excellent punter. His punts in the second half of the Wisconsin game were well placed, and he repelled the Badger attack by keeping them fighting down on their twenty-yard line. He gets his punts away fast and they are always high. He never seems to be hurried and has not had one punt blocked this season.

"In addition, Britton is the best place kicker in the conference. Not only do his place kicks have accuracy, but they have more distance than anyone who has been kicking in late years in the conference. His place kicks are also always away fast and none of them have been blocked this season. We can expect that when the Illini get past mid-field they will have a good chance to score by turning this Big Bertha loose at our goal posts.

"The Illinois line bucking attack is done entirely by Wally McIlwain and Heine Schultz, and cannot be taken lightly. Both of these boys are terrific line buckers, but due to having an excellent open field runner in Grange, Zuppke is not specializing in line attack to any great extent this year. They have discovered ground can be made easier and quicker by Grange on his end runs."

The special abilities of our key team members such as Captain Jim McMillen and "Windy" Miller, left and right tackles, respectively; Wally McIlwain, right halfback; Harry "Swede" Hall, quarterback; Earl Britton, fullback; Frank Rokusek, left end; V. Green, center; "Mush" Crawford and Dick Hall, left and right guards, respectively; Ted Richards and Stub Muhl, alternates at right end; and Heine Schultz and Rune Clark, substitute halfbacks, were individually discussed in the report.

McMillen and Rokusek were acknowledged to be the best in the conference at their positions. It was brought out that McIlwain had made considerable yardage in some games as a driver and plunger. He was especially commended for "terrific bucking in the Nebraska game against a team that has such a large and powerful line." Harry Hall was described as "the brains of the Illinois outfit, who in addition to being a good quarterback is an excellent interferer and blocker. Hall is not afraid to open up when it becomes necessary and is the type of field director who will use plays that are going good. When he gets Grange going on his end run stuff, he does not hesitate to use him."

About Britton, it was pointed out further: "His greatest value to the Illinois team is his wonderful defensive strength. He backs up the Illini line from a point two yards back and is a tower of strength on all line plays and end runs. Britton is today the best defensive fullback in the Conference."

The report described me in this manner: " 'Red' Grange. Weight about 170 lbs. 6 ft. or a little better. Tall, slender, big boned, big feet, shifty and elusive. Grange is Number 77 and is the life of the Illinois team. When Grange is in, the team is a world beater. Grange dashes for wide sweeping end runs, short cut-ins or slashes off tackle and an occasional cut-back over center. His sweeps around end are extremely spectacular. He is able to outspeed tacklers who come thru the line and once he is past the line of scrimmage, is the most difficult man to get down the Conference has seen in several years. His speed due to his long stride is very deceiving.

"In the Iowa game, Grange asserted himself and beat the Iowa team by his sheer ability to catch passes at any speed, angle or height. In the Wisconsin game, his showing simply astounded the scouts, for his runs were only stopped by the Wisconsin team forcing him out of bounds, and none of them were for less than 11 yards. In this game, Grange passed on two occasions; one from his running formation out to the side to McIlwain and another from the punt formation, a screen pass to Right End Ted Richards. It is also said that Grange kicks quite a bit, but due to the excellent way that Mr. Britton takes care of the kicking, it is highly improbable that Grange will do any punting.

"While Grange has shown remarkable speed, dodging, hip shift, stop up, change of pace, and other abilities, yet when he is caught by several tacklers, the man simply puts on steam and drives and whirls in an even better manner than Earl Martineau, the great Gopher, and leaves a wake of would-be tacklers strewn in his path behind him."

I strongly dispute the reference in the report to my big feet. I wear a size nine shoe today, as I did then, and this is actually small for a man of my size. The only way I can imagine I got the reputation for having big feet is that Zuppke speaking at a banquet earlier that season jokingly said, "Grange's big feet are two principal reasons for his being hard to knock down."

Certain minor weaknesses in our defensive play were also noted and brought out in the report. However, for the most part there was nothing but high praise for our all-round team play. "The team is extremely high-class in end running, kicking, place kicking, bucking, and passing and pass receiving on the offense. They have a good line, good secondary defenders and tacklers on the defense. Their punt receiving is well taken care of by a dangerous man and their punt covering ably done by two good ends and the center on the first wave and a tenacious line and backfield coming down on the second wave. The administration of their plays and attack is high-class and their blocking interference is good. Thus, it would seem that Illinois is a really good team, with no really great outstanding weakness."

It concluded in the do-or-die college spirit. "To beat this team we will have to rise to heights that we have not risen to before and stop this super attack. We shall simply have to beat down their defense by a terrific, more than just ordinary man power, offense. Our team must play—and can play—this way if they key themselves up to desperation. This is the only type of football that will beat the Illini."

As I said earlier, when Illinois played the Buckeyes in Columbus on November 24, 1923, we had a real battle on our hands even though we won 9-0. It is clear Ohio State made good use of the information gained from their scouting report on us.

6

Four Touchdowns in Twelve Minutes

THE ILLINOIS VS. MICHIGAN GAME of October 18, 1924, actually began many months before the opening kickoff. We hadn't played the Wolverines the previous season, but wound up sharing the 1923 conference title with five victories and no defeats apiece. With justifiable pride each school eagerly looked forward to this game as the acid test to determine which team was really the champion. But Michigan and her athletic director, Fielding Yost, didn't actually consider us a serious threat. They figured on beating us handily and made the point well known to the press.

No sooner had school let out in June when Zup started to go to work on getting us keyed up for the impending contest. Throughout the summer vacation he sent a continuous flow of letters to me and the rest of the team about how Michigan expected to romp over us. By the time we returned to the campus for the fall semester we were all so mad that beating the Yostmen from Ann Arbor became the most important issue in our lives.

One of the things Zup wrote us about concerned

the plans Yost had for me. When asked by a reporter, "What about Grange?" Michigan's headman answered, "Mr. Grange will be a carefully watched man every time he takes the ball. There will be just about eleven clean, hard Michigan tacklers headed for him at the same time. I know he is a great runner, but great runners usually have the hardest time gaining ground when met by special preparation."

The special preparation Yost had in mind was to encourage my assuming an offensive role as frequently as possible so I could be hit hard and often and eventually worn down. This strategy made sense from Michigan's viewpoint. It worked successfully the year before when the Wolverines bottled up Earl Martineau, Minnesota's great running halfback.

During the summer I worked hard at becoming a passer. Zup gave me several footballs to take home and practice with. He stressed the importance of my developing into a passer so the opposition would not be sure when I took the ball whether I would pass or run with it. This way I could increase my effectiveness as a runner and also make my work easier.

I started out by winging baseballs to my brother Garland for hours at a time until I developed near-perfect control and the ability to throw on the run. Then I switched to throwing a football. It got so I could pass with a high degree of accuracy at twenty or thirty yards.

Zup's determination to make a passer out of me might have had something to do an opinion expressed by the University of Michigan's student paper following my sophomore season in 1923.

When the *Michigan Daily* picked an All-American eleven that year, I only rated a berth on the second team. That experts like Walter Camp and Walter Eckersall regarded me a unanimous choice for All-American halfback did not alter their selection. The Michigan organ claimed: "All Grange can do is run." Zup defended my honor with the reply: "All Galli-Curci can do is sing." It is true, however, that up until my junior year I was strictly a runner. But running does win football games and I tried my darnedest to prove that to Michigan when we played them.

The day before the Michigan encounter our team was quartered as usual at the Champaign Country Club where we held final drills on the soft turf in front of the clubhouse. Afterward, at dinner, we ate large portions of rare steak then settled back to relax in secluded luxury. It had been a tough, grueling week putting the finishing touches on our attack for Michigan, but now we felt ready for the important game we had pointed to for nearly five months.

On the eve of battle Zup did his customary job of bolstering our confidence and keeping us in high spirits. We never really knew how worried he was about the condition of two of his key blockers. Captain Frank Rokusek, the left end, still had the leg injury that kept him out of the Butler contest the week before, and Right Halfback Wallie McIlwain had to be put to bed with a stomach disorder. Although we had little difficulty defeating Nebraska and Butler in the first two games of the season, Zup's anxiety was not relieved. He knew the Wolverines would be tough and wanted to win against them in the worst way.

The Michigan contest was the occasion of the dedication of the University of Illinois' mammoth Memorial Stadium. Over 67,000 fans were on hand and it was estimated 20,000 more were unable to get in. It was the largest crowd ever assembled in the Midwest for a football game.

There were impressive pre-game ceremonies including a dedication speech by Illinois' President David Kinley and a parade of students who were ex-servicemen. At the conclusion a bugler blew taps for the Illini who lost their lives in World War I. Thousands of fans in Chicago unable to see the proceedings and the game which followed, got Sportscaster Quinn Ryan's eye-witness account via radio station WGN. It marked the first time an Illinois football game had been broadcast.

The playing field was in perfect condition. Resembling a well-kept golf fairway, it was a beautiful emerald green. The day was clear and sunny. Typical Indian-summer weather, but much too warm for football.

As we sat around in the locker room listening to last-minute instructions before game time, Zup suddenly turned to assistant coach Justa Lindgren and asked, "Anything in the rule book that says we can't remove our stockings?" A quick look revealed no such regulation. "Okay fellas, let's take off the stockings. It's hot out there and without those heavy socks you'll feel a lot fresher and cooler."

We were stunned at Zup's odd request and momentarily balked at the idea. A football team had never before appeared in a game without full-length stockings. We were afraid we'd get our legs skinned and scratched without them. But when Zup barked, "C'mon, let's get going we don't have much time left," we peeled them off in fast order.

When we trotted out on the field for the start of the game, Director Yost and his coach George Little immediately spotted our bare legs and became suspicious. Since we had worn our stockings in the pre-game practice they figured this was a Zuppke trick. That in desperation to win we had put grease on our legs so we could not be tackled low.

Yost and Little protested to the officials, but after consultation the latter agreed there was nothing they could do about it. Continuing to make an issue of the possibility our legs were greased, it was suggested they find out for themselves.

In full view of the tremendous crowd, Yost ordered Coach Little and the Michigan team captain, Herb Steger, to feel the legs of the Illinois players for grease. An inspection of the entire team naturally revealed nothing but hair and muscle on our lower extremities.

Throughout their long and brilliant careers a great personal rivalry existed between Bob Zuppke and Fielding Yost, and each always regarded the other with suspicion.

In 1922, when Illinois last played host to Michigan, Zup found a penny on the locker-room floor shortly before game time. Thinking it might bring his team luck he put the coin in his pocket. When the Illini went down in defeat 24-0, Zup began having his doubts about that penny.

By coincidence, Zup again found a one-cent piece on the floor of the locker room the day of this latest Michigan-Illinois contest. He was now convinced it was Yost who in each case planted the copper coin for bad luck. Accordingly Zup wasted little time in hurling the supposed charm out of the window.

Getting back to Zuppke's bare legs innovation, when the defiant Wolverines were convinced no trickery was involved, they finally took the field. Illinois' Captain Rokusek won the toss and elected to receive with Michigan defending the south goal. The first stockingless football game in history was on.

Steger of Michigan kicked off deep, and I caught the ball on the fly in front of the goal posts on our five-yard line. Running straight down center, I cut wide to the right to avoid a host of tacklers at about the thirty-yard line. From the extreme west side I cut back across the field and headed up the east sidelines, crossing the goal line just a fraction of a second after Wolverine quarterback Tod Rockwell made a frantic dive to get me. Earl Britton kicked the extra point and we led 7-0.

Michigan's next kickoff was again long and I carried fifteen yards to our twenty-yard line. Illinois was penalized for illegal use of the hands. On the next play

McIlwain bucked for two yards, then Britton got off a short punt to our own thirty-five-yard line. Rockwell of Michigan passed to the fullback Miller for nine yards and the latter added two more on the next play for a first down. Steger gained two more yards through left tackle but lost two on another attempt through the right side of the line. A forward pass by Rockwell was incomplete. On fourth down, after fumbling a place kick, Rockwell was trapped and thrown for a loss on our thirty-yard line.

After we took over the ball on downs, McIlwain hit right guard for a three-yard gain. On the next play I got away for another score as I stepped around left end, cut back, then circled behind my interference. When Britton made the extra point we led 14-0.

I took Steger's third kickoff and ran it back to our twenty-yard line where I was tackled by the left guard Slaughter. After a five-yard penalty against Michigan for an offside, I picked up seven yards through right tackle. Britton punted sixty yards on third down and Rokusek downed the ball on Michigan's twenty-yard line. After a two-yard gain by Steger, Rockwell kicked back to our forty-three-yard line.

Following McIlwain's plunge through left tackle for a yard, I was given the ball on Illinois' forty-four-yard line and took off around right end. When my blockers allowed the Michigan secondary to get outside of them, I cut back to the center of the field where I had a clear path to the goal line. Britton missed the point after touchdown and the score was Illinois 20, Michigan 0.

When Steger kicked off for the fourth time the ball sailed beyond the goal and we took over on our twenty-yard line. Trying to break through the right side of the line, I was thrown for a five-yard loss. Britton then got off a long punt that was taken by Rockwell, but when he fumbled Rokusek recovered on Michigan's forty-five-yard line.

On the next play we tried the identical maneuver that resulted in my last touchdown. Running wide around right end I cut back when the Michigan secondary was again drawn over to the sidelines. After side-stepping a few stray would-be tacklers in mid-field, I found easy sailing to another tally. Britton's kick was good and we led 27-0.

The fifth kickoff by Steger was taken by McIlwain and he advanced the ball to our twenty-seven-yard line. McIlwain then smacked through left tackle for seven yards and I got loose for nineteen more around right end. The latter play was nullified when we were penalized five yards for being offside.

Rockwell momentarily fumbled Britton's forty-five-yard punt, but recovered on the Wolverines' twenty-eight-yard line. At this juncture our quarterback, Harry "Swede" Hall, called for a time out.

When Matt Bullock, the Illinois trainer, came in with the water, he asked me how I felt. I answered truthfully, "I'm so dog-tired I can hardly stand up. Better get me outa here." With three minutes left in the first quarter, Zup obliged by sending Ray Gallivan in to replace me.

As I trotted wearily off the field the crowd cheered

wildly. They continued to yell, stamp and applaud for several minutes. I was grateful for their acclaim, but much too exhausted to fully appreciate the thrill of such a tribute.

Besides the four touchdown runs of ninety-five, sixty-seven, fifty-six and forty-five yards, I covered about another forty yards for a total of 303 yards in the first twelve minutes of play. Nevertheless, the first thing Zup said to me when I came over to the bench was: "Shoulda had another touchdown Red. You didn't cut at the right time on that last play." That was typical of the psychology Zup always used on his players to prevent their becoming cocky or overconfident.

Against Michigan I cut back for the first time in my college career, and it was the greatest single factor in my being able to break away consistently for long runs. In planning their defense, the Wolverines counted on my following the pattern of my sophomore season and the game with Butler the week previous. That pattern was to head straight down the sidelines after skirting an end. When I discarded that style of running and used the cut back, Michigan had no defense worked out to cope with it.

However, it is a fact the success I enjoyed at the expense of Michigan could not have been accomplished without the powerful blocking of Rokusek, Hall, Britton, McIlwain and the rest of the Illinois team. Also, I have always felt the confusion that resulted when we appeared on the field without stockings enabled us to get the jump on the disturbed Yostmen before they settled down.

I remained out of the game the entire second quarter. Steger scored and Rockwell kicked the extra point for Michigan in that period and at half time we were ahead 27-7. Between halves all was quiet and calm in the locker room despite our sizable lead over the proud Wolverines. Just as always, Zup went about the serious business of pointing out our mistakes and plotted our defenses for the second half of the contest.

In the third period I threw three passes good for eighteen yards and accounted for eighty-five yards by rushing, including a touchdown from the Wolverines' twelve-yard line. Britton's kick for the extra point was wide. The scoreboard read Illinois –33, Michigan –7 at the end of the quarter.

The Michigan defense tightened considerably as the game progressed, but midway in the fourth period I shot a short pass from their eighteen-yard line to Marion Leonard, McIlwain's substitute at right halfback, and he went over for another tally. Britton missed the kick again and it was 39-7.

The Wolverines scored their second touchdown late in the final quarter when a foul called against us on Steger's kickoff gave them possession of the ball on our thirteen-yard line. From there Steger went over after three consecutive attempts and Rockwell added the point after touchdown making the final score 39-14.

Bedlam broke loose in our locker room after the game. The place was jam-packed with excited reporters and photographers. Everyone was yelling, jumping up and down and running around slapping everyone else on the back. All I wanted to do was lie down and rest, but the newspapermen proceeded to surround me and ask an endless number of questions. It was nearly an hour after all the other players had departed before I was able to tear myself away. Even then I found it necessary to leave by a side door to avoid a large number of Illini rooters waiting for me on the outside.

When I got back to the fraternity house the place was in an uproar. The walls were literally bulging with alums, friends, Zeta Psi's from the Michigan chapter and more newspapermen. Escaping from all this posed a greater problem for me than eluding Michigan tacklers.

Finally, I managed to get up to my room and, after changing clothes, slipped out the kitchen door with one of my more understanding fraternity brothers. We had dinner by ourselves, then took in a movie. Returning about ten-thirty that night and finding conditions somewhat more peaceful, I went straight to bed.

7

My Toughest College Game

BEFORE OUR ROUSING VICTORY over Michigan, we opened the 1924 season with a 9-6 conquest of Nebraska, thanks to a field goal by Earl Britton, and the following week blasted Butler 40-0. In the Butler contest I tallied twice in the sixteen minutes I played, as did Ray Gallivan who replaced me. The week after we stopped the Wolverines 39-14, we trounced De Pauw 45-0. I didn't get into the De Pauw fracas but returned to action a week later when we humbled Iowa 36-0. Against the Hawkeyes I carried the ball thirty-seven times, scoring twice and racking up a total of 186 yards. My longest runs in that game were eighteen, nineteen and twenty yards. I also threw three passes that netted eighty-six yards.

With four straight wins under our belts we prepared to meet the University of Chicago eleven at Stagg Field on Saturday, November 8th. Up to that date the Maroons had defeated Indiana and Purdue and were held to a tie by Ohio State. Earlier in the season they won from Brown, but lost to Missouri in nonconference tilts. On the strength of the two records, Illinois was installed as a 3-1 favorite to whip Chicago.

Coach Amos Alonzo Stagg had his Chicago warriors pointing to the Illinois game all season just as we pointed to Michigan. The Maroons were highly keyed up for us while the psychological peak we attained in the clash with the Wolverines was fast on the downgrade. They were also out to revenge the 7-0 licking Illinois handed them the previous season. No one knew better what we were up against than our coach, Bob Zuppke. The day before the battle he gloomily told the press, "It is impossible for me to key up my team, unless, of course, it should lose a game. Right now Chicago has all the advantage. That team can be keyed up to play us, while all I can do is ask my team to show the pep it showed against Michigan and Iowa. You see," he continued, "a team under intensive coaching about this time begins to lose team interest. Too much is taken for granted and a squad is likely to slump if it runs into a bit of bad luck."

The Illinois-Chicago rivalry which began in 1892 always attracted great interest. The 1924 meeting of the two teams, which was the occasion of Chicago's Homecoming, was sold out weeks in advance. On the day of battle, forty thousand fans jammed Stagg Field to its absolute capacity. Many more thousands milled around the streets outside the stadium's walls hoping to pick up scalped tickets at the last minute. Scalpers were asking and getting from twenty dollars to one hundred dollars per ticket, but there just weren't enough to go around. For the benefit of those unable to gain admittance, several students perched themselves on the walls of Stagg Field and boomed the details of the game through megaphones.

Coach Stagg thought he had the perfect strategy to stop Illinois. Unlike Fielding Yost's plan for his Michigan squad, the Chicago mentor instructed his players to press for the offensive from the opening whistle and do everything possible to keep us from getting our hands on the ball. He figured his best chance for victory were if his forwards could outplay our line and open up holes through tackle or guard for the Maroon's great fullback plays. With a line that outweighed Illinois by almost fifteen pounds per man and boasting three of the conference's best linemen in Captain Franklin Gowdy and Joe Pondelick at guards and Bob Henderson at tackle, Stagg was on the right track.

The game started with Chicago winning the toss and electing to defend the south goal. Earl Britton kicked off and the Maroons brought the ball up to their twenty-eight-yard line. From that point on, Illinois had possession of the ball for just one play in the first period when Britton kicked after Austin McCarty, the busy Maroon fullback, fumbled on our ten-yard marker. McCarty plunged for practically all of his team's yardage until he fumbled and continued making steady gains when the Maroons took over again following Britton's punt. He finally went over for Chicago's first score and little Bob Curley, the Marcons' 135-pound quarterback, converted with a drop kick. In that opening quarter McCarty carried the ball fourteen times for a total of eighty-three yards.

The first quarter ended with Chicago ahead 7-0 and the ball resting on our one-yard line. On the first play of the second period Right Halfback Harry Thomas crashed through for his team's second tally. Curley, faking another drop kick, passed to the right end, Harrison Barnes, in the end zone, and Chicago led 14-0.

Illinois finally got the opportunity to assume an offensive role when we elected to receive after the Stagg men's second touchdown. Beginning a march from our twenty-five-yard line, where Illinois' quarterback Harry Hall brought Chicago's kickoff, we worked our way to our first touchdown. In that scoring drive I toted the pigskin five times for twenty yards, threw three passes good for forty-seven yards and went over for the tally. When Britton booted the extra point, the score stood 14-7 in favor of Chicago.

In the latter half of the second quarter, both teams scored again. Chicago crossed the goal line first and we scored minutes later in a drive that began from our twenty-six-yard line. I made the second touchdown after carrying the ball nine times from scrimmage for forty yards and catching two passes that accounted for forty-four yards. As both Chicago and Illinois added the kicks after touchdown, the Maroons led 21-14 at half time.

In the locker room between halves, Zuppke used all his powers of salesmanship and psychology to get us back into the game. He made us ashamed, sore and determined. I particularly remember the reference he made to the first quarter defensive play of our usually dependable fullback Earl Britton who absorbed considerable punishment yet was helpless in backing up the line against those powerful fullback thrusts of McCarty. Zup said to him, "What were you doing out there, Britton? You looked just like a guy standing up on the field playing a piano. Instead of hitting those guys hard you were pushing them away with your finger tips." Britton got so sore at Zup's remark he almost fractured the first Maroon who came his way at the start of the second half.

Early in the third period Illinois tied the score at 21-21 when I raced eighty yards for a touchdown. Taking the pigskin on the first play, after a Chicago punt to our twenty-yard marker, I shot around left end and down the side lines, then cut back through a maze of tacklers toward the center of the field and over the goal line. Britton added the extra point. Later that same quarter, McCarty, who remained out of the game the second period, returned to action and picked up seventeen yards in three attempts. In the fourth quarter, the 176-pound McCarty continued to pile up yardage by plowing through the line four times for another eighteen yards. No one could stop him. He was a battering ram that day if I ever saw one. It seemed that every time McCarty carried the ball he made at least five yards. For his brilliant work against Illinois, the Maroon fullback was nicknamed Five Yards McCarty, and gained football immortality.

With both teams tied going into the final period, the pressure was really on. Early in the quarter I made a thirty-three-yard dash around right end and a few plays later added nine more, but we eventually lost the ball on downs. Then, in the last few minutes of the game, with Chicago threatening, our right end, Chuck Kassel, intercepted an enemy pass on our ten-yard line. On the next play I took the ball and set out in a wide circle around left end and went fifty-one yards before being forced out of bounds by Bob Curley. With what seemed like a first down on Chicago's thirty-nine-yard line and nearly two minutes of playing time remaining, Illinois fans went wild at the prospect of our winning the hard-fought battle with a touchdown or a field goal. But the cheers soon turned to bitter moans when Illinois was penalized for offensive holding and my run was nullified. Instead of lining up on the Maroons' thirty-nine-yard line, we found ourselves on our one-yard marker as a result of the penalty. That ended any chance we might have had for victory. We fought desperately to regain the precious lost yardage, but all we could do this time was get up to the sixteen-yard line where Britton was forced to kick on fourth down. As his punt sailed into the air, the gun went off and the game ended in a 21-21 tie.

The Illinois-Chicago classic of 1924 was the toughest football game I ever played in college. Every time I was tackled I was hit hard by two or three men. At one point in the game I was so exhausted I fell flat on my face as the Maroons were running off a play. I was no exception, for the entire Illinois team took a terrific beating. I don't believe the Illini in my day had ever been in such a ferocious football game. Chicago, as I said earlier in this chapter, was a big, bruising team that played no open football. They would simply concentrate on plowing through tackle or guard with those overpowering fullback plays. In fact, they didn't attempt one pass in their clash with us. Illinois' offense, on the other hand, was based on deception. We tried to deceive the ends and line backers by pulling them out of position. It was a great study in contrasting football strategies.

One week after facing Chicago, a battered, weary band of Illinois athletes traveled up to Minneapolis to play Minnesota. The Gophers had yet to win their first conference game, having lost two and tied one. A victory over Illinois could salvage an otherwise dismal season. Led by Left Halfback Clarence Schutte, who made all of his team's touchdowns, Minnesota waged a hard, aggressive battle and walloped us 20-7. Illinois' lone tally came early in the first period when I swept ten yards around right end after we had marched from the Gophers' forty-two-yard stripe. Although I rang up our only score, I was completely bottled up in that contest. I figured in about twelve plays, but failed to make much yardage. The Minnesota encounter was just too much for us after what we had been through against Michigan and Chicago. In the third period a severe shoulder injury forced me to retire from the game. I hurt the shoulder when a Gopher player piled on me after I had intercepted a Minnesota pass and was thrown out of bounds. Harry

66

Hall, our quarterback, had to be taken out at the start of the second quarter when he hurt his collarbone. Following my injury and a resultant Minnesota penalty, I stayed in the game for two more plays. First I completed an eleven-yard pass, but when I attempted to throw again couldn't get the ball away and was knocked for a nine-yard loss. My arm felt limp and I couldn't raise it. Zup, noticing something was wrong, immediately signaled our quarterback to call time. Trotting out on the field, trainer Matt Bullock took one look at me and ordered me out of the contest. The injury was serious enough to keep me out of the season's finale with Ohio State the following week.

While we played Minnesota, Chicago was battling it out against Northwestern at Stagg Field. They were tied 0-0 near the end of the last quarter when the Maroons' coach sent in a sub to notify Quarterback Bob Curley that the Gophers were giving Illinois a shellacking. That did it. Fully aware that a victory over the Purple meant they stood a good chance of taking the Big Ten title, Chicago worked desperately to rack up a score They got as far as Northwestern's twenty-two-yard line when Curley put himself on the spot by electing to try for a field goal. Despite the tremendous pressure of the moment, he executed a perfect drop kick that cut the uprights in half. Curley's kick not only won the game for Chicago 3 to 0, but ultimately the undisputed Conference Championship. For although Illinois licked Ohio State 7-0 the next week and Chicago was held to a tie by Wisconsin, the Maroons' record of three wins, no losses and three ties was still the best percentage in the conference. Illinois was the runner-up with three wins, one loss and one tie. Counting our three nonconference games, our over-all record for the 1924 season was six wins, one loss and one tie.

At the close of my junior year I had accounted for thirteen touchdowns and seventy-eight points in the six games I participated in, to lead the Big Ten in scoring for the second straight year. In naming me again for his All-American squad, Walter Camp generously wrote:

Harold Grange is the marvel of this year's (1924) backfield. His work in the Michigan game was a revelation, but his performance in the Chicago game went even further when by his play—running and forward passing—he accounted for some 450 yards of territory. He is elusive, has a baffling change of pace, a good straight arm and finally seems in some way to get a map of the field at starting and then threads his way through his opponents.

8

Illinois Invades the East

ILLINI ROOTERS had little to look forward to at the start of the 1925 season. Coach Zuppke summed up the problem that faced us that year when he told reporters, "It's going to be some job to fill the places of the experienced players who were lost to us by graduation." The players he referred to were Frank Rokusek, captain and end of the 1924 squad, Dick Hall, tackle, Lou Slimmer and Roy Miller, guards, Gil Roberts, center, and Wallie McIlwain and Heinie Schultz, backs. To make matters worse, Harry Hall, our star quarterback for the past two seasons, could not be counted on for regular duty due to the injury he received to his collarbone in the Minnesota battle. My brother Garland, who had been a standout halfback on the freshman team in 1924 and was expected to win a regular berth on the varsity, withdrew from school shortly before the season got under way as a result of an injury sustained in practice.

The only returning regulars in the line were Chuck Brown at right tackle and Stub Muhl and Chuck Kassel, ends. Besides the handicapped Harry Hall, Earl Britton and I were the only backfield starters around from the previous campaign, yet Zup was forced to shift Britton from his fullback spot to right guard in a frantic attempt to bolster the strength of the forward wall. Small wonder the 1925 eleven was the poorest team Illinois had had in several seasons. Having been elected captain my senior year, I had the dubious honor of leading my team to what everyone thought would be the slaughter.

With a green squad composed mostly of sophomores and substitutes from the year before, Illinois lost three out of their first four games. Our initial defeat was suffered on opening day, October 3rd, at the hands of Nebraska. Losing by a 14-0 score, it was the first time we had been beaten in our new stadium. We came back to whip a weak Butler team the following week, 16-13, then lost two in a row to Iowa and Michigan by scores of 12-10 and 3-0. Finding myself running with little or no interference, I was completely bottled up in the Nebraska and Michigan games, but fared somewhat better against Butler and Iowa. I scored twice in the Butler contest, the first one on a seventy-yard run, while against the Hawkeyes I ran back the opening kickoff eighty-five yards for a touchdown.

The Michigan battle of 1925 was an especially tough one for me personally. Because of what I had done to them the previous season, I was a marked man. The entire Wolverine defense was geared to stop me and they did a good job of it with the aid of a sloppy turf. I particularly remember Benny Friedman, Michigan's great quarterback, sticking to me that entire afternoon like flypaper. Friedman, incidentally, won the game for Michigan by booting a twenty-five-yard field goal in the second period. I played quarterback for the first time in this contest and remained at that position the rest of the season. Zup had approached me several weeks earlier and said, "Red, I think you should move to quarterback. If you call signals I think the boys will have confidence in you." The Illinois coach worked with me many long hours until I was ready to take on my new assignment. Preparing me for my role as a quarterback he taught me things about football I had never even thought of before. It was a rich, rewarding experience learning the intricacies of football strategy from the Dutch Master.

One week, after being nosed out by Michigan 3-0, Illinois prepared to invade the East and pit our supposedly waning strength against one of the greatest football aggregations in that section of the country, the University of Pennsylvania. On the face of our record thus far in the season, nobody figured we had even a fighting chance to win. Penn had already beaten Ursinus, Swarthmore, Brown and mighty Yale. They had subdued Chicago 7-0 the previous week. The most conservative predictions had Penn swamping us by four or five touchdowns.

We faced the Quakers from Pennsylvania on Saturday, October 31st at Franklin Field, Philadelphia. It was a cold, damp day, since it rained and snowed almost the entire night before. The playing field, with nothing more than straw to protect it from the elements, was like a big mud cake. Despite the bad

71

weather conditions, 65,000 fans wearing heavy over-coats, furs and overshoes crowded into the stadium for one of the largest turnouts ever to see a sporting event in Philadelphia. All of the important eastern sports writers such as Grantland Rice, Ed Pollock, David Walsh, Harry Gross, Damon Runyon and Ford Frick were on hand to give their readers eye-witness accounts of the battle. There was more than the usual amount of interest generally connected with an inter-sectional clash of this kind. I think many people were just downright curious to find out whether there was anything to the reputation I had established playing against football teams in the Midwest.

Illinois started preparing for the Penn game late in the 1924 season when Zup asked us at practice one night, "You boys who will be back next year—how would you like to play the University of Pennsylvania on their home grounds in Philadelphia?" When we shouted our approval he added, "All right, I'll see what I can do." The fact is, the game had already been scheduled, but that was Zup's way of stirring up in-terest in his charges.

During the summer, after the players had been def-initely informed of the impending battle with Penn, Zuppke followed the identical procedure that proved so successful against Michigan in 1924. He sent many personal letters to all of us on the squad telling how the eastern teams looked down their noses at midwest-ern football and that it was our duty to demonstrate to the football world that we were every bit as good or better than they. Zup also wrote that he had discovered a sure way to defeat the feared Quakers and all we had to do was report for fall practice in good shape and he'd show us how. He succeeded in getting us so keyed up for the Penn game that even our miserable showing in the 1925 season prior to our appearance in Philly didn't take the edge off our determination to beat the easterners.

Zup's battle plan for Penn, based on an exhaustive study of the most reliable scouting reports, was a comparatively simple yet brilliant one: he deduced the only possible way of winning over such a powerful eleven was on weak side plays. To explain what our coach meant, it is necessary to know that Illinois used a single wing offense with an unbalanced line that would shift to the right with four linemen on the right side of center and two on the left side of center. On a shift to the left the same formation would apply in that direction. Now Zup found out that Penn always overshifted on defense—which meant they practically put their entire defense on the side where the shift went, leaving the weak side of the offensive formation practically unguarded. So he told me to call as many plays around the weak side as possible without establishing a definite pattern. His specific instructions before the game were: "In the first two plays of the game run Britton through the strong side. On the third play line up strong on the short side of the field and you take the ball around the weak side."

The Penn-Illinois battle began with the Quakers kicking off and my returning the ball to our thirty-six-yard line. Just as the coach had ordered, I had

Britton take the ball on the first two plays through the strong side, and he got brutally smeared. After the second unsuccessful attempt he said to me in the huddle, "Say, what have you against me?" Britton then punted and when Penn also failed to gain, they kicked back and Illinois wound up with the ball on their forty-yard line. On the very next play we lined up strong to the right and I took the ball around the left and raced fifty-five yards to a touchdown without encountering a single Penn player all the way. We continued mixing weak side plays with strong side plays for the rest of the first half and it netted us two more touchdowns. Earl Britton and Left Halfback Pug Daugherity were used mostly as decoys to run around the strong side, but I, too, ran the strong side on occasion to confuse the opposition. Our second touchdown came minutes later in the first quarter when Britton went over from the one-yard stripe. We started that march when I took the second Penn kick-off on my twenty and ran it back fifty-five yards to the Quaker twenty-five-yard line. At this point in the game the field was a veritable quagmire with both the Penn and Illinois players covered with mud from head to foot. The numbers and features of all of us were almost indistinguishable in the gooey mess.

Illinois scored its third touchdown late in the second quarter as I skirted twelve yards to the goal around left end. It was early in that same period that Penn scored their only two points of the game on a safety when Britton fell on his blocked punt as it bounded behind our goal post.

Between halves, Coach Louis A. Young of the Penn team told his players not to shift so much on defense, but it was too late; Illinois had taken the starch out of them. In the third period we scored our fourth and last touchdown. We led up to it when Britton and Daugherity rolled up consistent yardage plowing through center and I accounted for some thirty-nine yards through tackle and dashes around end. With the ball on Penn's twenty-yard line I decided to try Zuppke's tricky flea flicker play. Seeing what I was up to, Zup quickly jumped off the bench—which was the signal to call off a play. When I paid no attention to him, he excitedly sent in a substitute with orders to change the play, but I waved the player back to the bench. Before Zup could take any drastic action, I was calling the signals. Completely frustrated at this point, he turned his back to the team and held his hands over his eyes. Zuppke's flea flicker play was now on. I knelt on one knee eight yards behind the center like I was going to hold the ball for Earl Britton to place kick. Instead of going to me the oval was centered directly to Britton who immediately lobbed to Chuck Kassel, the right end. Without taking a step, Kassel just turned around and flipped me a lateral as I got up off the ground and ran about twenty yards to his right. I then made the twenty yards down field to the goal while the Penn defense did little more than gape in utter amazement. It was real razzle-dazzle football and it worked just like you draw it out on the blackboard. I think it would still be a great play if tried today. Funny thing—that night after the game Zup told

75

a band of admirers in the lobby of the Benjamin Franklin Hotel that he planned for months to use that flea flicker play in precisely that kind of spot in the ball game.

When Pennsylvania and Illinois failed to score in the last quarter, the contest ended in a 24-2 win for our team. I left the game with about five minutes left in the final quarter after picking up another fifty-three yards in four attempts. On one play I scooted around left end for forty yards before being thrown out of bounds. When it was all over I had had probably the best day of my collegiate football career. I made 363 yards in thirty-six tries, figuring in the two runs of fifty-five yards and the one for forty, and scored three times. The newspapers were most kind and generous in their reports of the game. Damon Runyon paid me an especially fine compliment when he wrote: "This man Red Grange of Illinois is three or four men and a horse rolled into one for football purposes. He is Jack Dempsey, Babe Ruth, Al Jolson, Paavo Nurmi and Man o' War. Put them all together, they spell Grange."

There were many factors responsible for our surprising showing against Penn. First and foremost was the brilliant strategy engineered by Zuppke that called for our using weak side plays against the Quakers. This probably more than any other single factor was responsible for our unexpected victory. Then there was the psychological build-up Zup gave us. Our team was at its absolute peak for that game as we were against Michigan in 1924. The line, which was com-

76

pletely helpless earlier in the campaign, functioned with machinelike precision. And it got stronger as the battle progressed. A popular saying of the time was "Penn rules the East," but after our second touchdown in the first quarter our linemen became so cocky they stood up before almost every play and shouted, "Illinois rules the East." Then they'd wildly charge in and bowl over the opposition.

The play of Pug Daugherity and Earl Britton in the backfield was also top rate. Daugherity clicked off from four to eight yards when yardage was needed and once got away for a twenty-five-yard run which helped set the stage for our fourth touchdown against the easterners. Britton, although he surprisingly missed all four points after touchdown, was ever dependable on defense, and hit the line with more viciousness than I'd ever seen him do before. His punting average of thirty-seven yards was most remarkable considering the sloppy footing and slippery ball. Twice the burly fullback kicked over fifty yards.

Last, but not least, was the inspiration the team got when the magnificent 150-piece University of Illinois band performed in front of the stands just before the kickoff. Making a dramatic entrance onto the field at the last minute, since their train had been delayed en route, they electrified the crowd with their snappy formations and stirring music. There had never been anything to equal it on an eastern gridiron. We couldn't help but catch that "Fighting Illini" spirit.

Typical of some of the headlines that blazoned across the country as a result of our triumph over the team that was considered by many to be not only the best in the East but in the entire nation, were: "ILLINI TOPPLE QUAKERS, 24-2"; "CORN-LAND TEAM AND BAND STUPEFY QUAKER CITY"; "ILLINI AND 'RED' SCALP PENN, 24 TO 2"; "ILLINOIS BATTERS PENN INTO SUBMIS-SION, 24-2"; "SOGGY FIELD FAILS TO HALT GRANGE WHO RUNS PENN'S ENDS RAG-GED"; "GRANGE AND ILLINOIS BEAT PENN, 24-2." Back in Champaign the Illini supporters went wild with joy. When our train pulled into home port on Monday, twenty thousand students, faculty members and townfolk turned out at the station to greet the Illinois players. I tried to avoid the excitement by slipping out the last coach of the train, but the crowd swarmed all over me when someone spotted me and yelled, "There's Grange." I was hoisted on the shoulders of several fellow students and carried through the surging throng almost two miles down the streets to my fraternity house.

Illinois played three more games after the Penn debacle and won all of them. We took the first one from Chicago 13-6 on November 7th under weather conditions far worse than we encountered in Philadelphia. We had a sell-out crowd of 67,000 in Memorial Stadium as twenty-five special trains left Chicago loaded with Maroon rooters. I lost more ground than I made in that battle with Chicago. Every time I tried to run my feet went out from under me. It was a slippery mud unlike the kind we played in against Penn, and for a runner of my type, who did a lot of cutting, it was an impossible situation. Earl Britton was the Illinois hero that day. His touchdown and long punts were responsible for victory. Austin "Five Yards" McCarty was injured in the second period and had to leave the game, but he was still Chicago's best ground-gainer of the day. It was a hard-fought contest to the finish as were all games in the Illinois-Chicago series, but good sportsmanship prevailed at all times. Just one week before, Chicago's Coach A. A. Stagg telegraphed Illinois' Bob Zuppke after the Penn game. "Heartiest congratulations to you and Captain Grange and the Illinois team on your wonderful victory. You did what Chicago couldn't do, but Chicago along with the whole West rejoices in your glorious defense of the prestige of (Big Ten) Conference football."

After subduing Chicago, the Illini whipped Wabash 21 to 0. I entered the game for just three plays in the last quarter, but didn't carry the ball. It was my last appearance on our home grounds. Our final game of the season with Ohio State at Columbus ended in a 14-9 Illinois victory.

At season's end, Michigan and Northwestern tied for the 1925 conference title. Michigan won five and lost one, while Northwestern recorded only three wins against one loss, however the Wolverines' lone defeat was at the hands of the Purple. Chicago, the winner in 1924, sank to sixth place. Illinois tied with Iowa for fifth place with two wins and two defeats in conference competition, but our overall season's record was five wins and three losses. Our defeat of unbeaten Penn was the season's crowning point as far as Illini rooters were concerned. It made the 1925 season a complete success. As for myself, my six touchdowns in the 1925 season brought my three-year total at Illinois to thirty-one. Walter Camp died in March, 1925, but I was named on all the other All-American teams at the end of my senior year.

9

The Dutch Master

A BOOK BASED upon my life story would not be complete unless one chapter at least were devoted to the man who made me in football and who, next to my father, was perhaps the most important person in my life. That man, as you probably guessed, is my old coach and long-time friend, Robert C. Zuppke of Illinois.

Zup's record, over a period of twenty-eight seasons, in the Western Conference and against the big teams of the East and West, was one of the most outstanding in football. In 1914, his second season at Illinois, Zup gave the university its first undisputed championship of the Western Conference. And he accomplished this with a team that averaged 174 pounds, three of the regulars averaging only 146 pounds. When Zup retired at the end of the 1941 season, his teams had won and shared a total of seven Western Conference Championships. In addition he gained an impressive number of brilliant upsets in the nonchampionship years.

Perhaps the greatest upset victory of Zup's career was against Minnesota's "perfect team" on November 4, 1916. In that game the Illini were not given the slightest chance of winning. Earlier in the season the Gophers had soundly trounced Iowa 67-0, South Dakota 81-0, Chicago 49-0 and Wisconsin 53-0. Off that record the experts pretty generally predicted a 49-0 defeat for the Illini. All were proved utterly wrong, because of their failure to recognize Zuppke was at his best when cast in the underdog role. When the odds seemed hopeless Zup always took a long chance—he'd shoot the works to win rather than merely attempt to keep the score down.

The long chance Zup took in that game with Minnesota was the key factor in turning sure defeat into a rousing victory for the Illini. It took a stroke of genius to conceive such strategy and a very courageous individual to carry it out.

Several days before the clash with the Gophers, Zup told his hard-working squad, "This Minnesota outfit is superstitious and they've got a formula they always follow on the first three plays. First, Galloping Sprafka will carry the ball, next Wyman will carry it and, on the third play, Shorty Long will lug it. On the first three plays, tackle those men in that order."

One of the boys asked, "Suppose they cross us up? Suppose we gang up on those guys and someone else has the ball. What then?"

"If that happens," Zup answered, "I'll run out on the field and tackle the fellow with the ball myself."

Sure enough, when game time arrived and Minnesota received on the opening kickoff, Sprafka, Wyman and Long respectively carried the ball on the first three plays. Zup's plan worked like a charm. Each time they were smothered until the mighty Gophers were almost pushed back to their goal line.

Minnesota succeeded in kicking out of danger on fourth down, but never entirely recovered from the shock of being so completely overpowered in the first few seconds of play. On the other hand, the Illini became an inspired team. Taking charge from that point on, they finally wound up on the long end of an unbelievable 14-9 score.

Zuppke can rightly be referred to as the Edison of Football. His contributions to the fall sport have been many and varied. He invented the spiral pass from center, the huddle, started the practice of pulling both guards back from a balanced line to protect the forward passer and originated the "screen pass." Forward and lateral passes were part of his repertoire as far back as 1906, when he was coach of Muskegon High School. He was the originator of strategy maps, the most comprehensive guides for a quarterback I have ever seen.

Whenever Zup came up with a successful maneuver he gave it a colorful name so it would be easier for his players to remember.

The following is a list of some of the more famous Zuppke plays: the flea flicker; the blue eagle; the corkscrew; the sidewinder; the whirligig; the razzle-dazzle; the whoa back; the flying trapeze.

The "flea flicker" is the best known of all, and through the years Zup developed many variations of it. In our use of the play to score against Pennsylvania, it was worked from place-kick formation—a short forward pass to our right end who flicked a lateral to the left half as the latter went wide around right end.

With all his strategy and new innovations Zup never followed a so-called "system." Unlike many big-time coaches of his day, he merely adapted his coaching wizardry to his material and the talent of the men available. This flexibility was part of Zup's greatness.

Although his approach to football was highly scientific, Zup was by nature as superstitious as a tribal witch doctor. I get a chuckle when recalling two particular superstitions of his.

One had to do with his wearing of five rings on his right hand during the football season. He was constantly rotating the rings, sometimes wearing two or three on one finger, until his team started winning. When achieving victory, Zup partly attributed it to his having found the lucky combination.

Another superstition concerned his brother Herman of Minneapolis who made a habit of attending one important Illinois game each fall. For a gag, Herman always wore a striped orange and blue tie—representing Illinois' school colors—to the games and, by a strange coincidence, never saw an Illini team defeated. This went on for several years until Zup suddenly attached a connection between victory and his brother's tie. Arrangements were then made for the charmed tie to be left in a Champaign safety deposit vault and removed annually when Herman came to town to see the Illini play.

When it came to the psychology of football, the Dutch Master, as Zup was sometimes called, had no peers. His ideas on the subject could well form the basis of a coach's bible. I remember a talk I had with Zup several years after I left Illinois. Some of the things he told me that day may serve to illustrate the point.

"You may coach a college team sometime, Red," Zup said. "When and if you do, here are some things to remember. Your task will be to get the best out of your squad. To do so, you must deal with them as men. Cultivate their respect, confidence and good will by sincerity and absolute fairness. Be impersonal in your criticism of the whole squad and make your direct criticism to the player in private.

"Do not ridicule the scrubs. Treat each one alike, be he star or humble substitute. Insist on a high standard of accomplishment. Do not permit carelessness or indifference.

"Praise sparingly. If you overdo it, it will be meaningless. Be careful not to spank, then kiss. It will ruin discipline. You must be a developer of men as well as a selector of men. Keep your coaching simple and your English plain.

"Insist on absolute obedience to a reasonable common-sense set of training rules, and keep your squad in the correct mental attitude toward those rules. It is a matter of squad loyalty. Don't spy on the men. Place training rules before them as a matter of a gentlemen's agreement."

Zup emphasized: "Put this down in capital letters. A losing squad needs your help more than a winning team. Bolster their confidence. Let them know that you believe in them and will be with them—win, lose or draw. That is the true test of a coach—how he handles a team that simply hasn't the talent and ability to hold its own against bigger teams from a physical standpoint. If he can lift the boys beyond themselves, then he is a real coach. Victory in football is 40 per cent ability and 60 per cent spirit.

"Some years ago," he continued, "the coach of a small college team came to see me. His team hadn't won a game in five years. On the following Saturday his eleven was meeting a traditional rival. He was distraught and jittery.

"I said to him, 'Are your boys in shape? Have they got courage? Have you taught them sound football?'

"When he answered 'yes' to all of those questions, I told him, 'Go home and sleep like a baby. Let the other coach do the worrying. Think what will happen to his reputation if his team is the first one you beat in five years!' "

Resuming his convictions on coaching he went on: "Above all, be a gentleman in dealing with your squad. Remember that you are working with young men who deserve your best and who are critical of you.

"Football may be a brutal game, but brutes can't play it. It calls for sportsmanship, fairness and courtesy. And keep in mind courage is strictly an individual thing. It doesn't belong to any one nation or race. I have seen them all in my years of coaching. The longer I am in contact with every race and creed, the more I discover how little the human race differs."

Zup concluded: "A good coach makes better players out of good ones and often makes good players out of mediocre ones. He emphasizes their abilities, enables them to make the most of their latent talent, gives them the best chance by putting the right player in the right place.

"Many boys develop tremendously after a single season. For example, three of our All-American linemen: Slooey Chapman, Jim McMillen and Bernie Shively all were failures as sophomores.

"The work of the coach is more apparent when he deals with raw material. Then the team's progress is visible. But the coach shows his ability just as much when he polishes material that is already developed and fits it to the team. He superimposes good habits of play on bad ones.

"Players must have morale and loyalty, and the most important job of the coach is to instill this morale and loyalty, no matter what the material is. That is where his personality counts. The fawning, crawling, pleading coach neither leads nor directs. Boys follow a leader, but are herded in front of a driver. They are suspicious of the whip behind but look with trust to the man in front."

No matter what cause Zup had to become impatient or aggravated at a particular moment, I never knew him to use abusive language on a player. If a boy made a costly mistake in a game, or failed to follow instructions on the practice field, Zup would look him straight in the eye and say, "You lemon, you!" When the Dutch Master used this expression, he

87

didn't have to say another word to get his point across.

Zup was a supersalesman and a great humorist. He could "fire" his team to any pitch and had the uncanny knack of making a funny remark at precisely the right psychological moment to relieve tension.

Because of the methods employed in handling his team personnel, I believe football was always at its best under the Zuppke banner. To Zup football was more than just a game to win or lose. It was a means to build character. Because a little bit of Illinois' immortal coach rubbed off on all his charges, a boy who played under the Dutch Master stood every chance of emerging a winner, regardless of whether or not he performed on a championship eleven.

Wheaton High School football team, 1920. Grange is in the first row, third from the left. Courtesy of Wheaton College Special Collections.

Memorial Stadium opening day, Homecoming, November 3, 1923. Attendance was estimated at 67,000. Courtesy of the University of Illinois Archives, Record Series 39/2/20.

Grange shows off his passing form at Illinois. Courtesy of the University of Illinois
Sports Information Office.

Grange with Coach Robert Zuppke. Courtesy of the University of Illinois Sports Information Office.

"RED" GRANGE STARTS FOR THE GOAL LINE
ILLINOIS 39 — MICHIGAN 14
1924

Grange (far left) in action against Michigan, at the dedication of Memorial Stadium, October 18, 1924. Courtesy of the University of Illinois Sports Information Office.

University of Illinois varsity football team, 1924. Grange is in the second row, first on the left. Courtesy of the University of Illinois Archives, Record Series 39/2/20.

A posed photo of Grange from about 1925. Courtesy of the University of Illinois Archives, Record Series 39/2/20.

A publicity still of Grange pitching for the Illinois baseball team. Courtesy of the University of Illinois Sports Information Office.

Grange at the coin toss of the Illinois-Ohio State game, November 21, 1925.
Courtesy of the University of Illinois Archives, Record Series 39/2/20.

Grange and his jersey, after his last Illinois game. Courtesy of the University of Illinois Sports Information Office.

Two sports legends: Grange with Babe Ruth, taken in 1925 while Grange was playing for the Chicago Bears. Courtesy of the University of Illinois Sports Information Office.

Grange in his Chicago Bears uniform, in 1931. Courtesy of Ira
Morton.

Grange broadcasting an Illinois game for CBS radio. Courtesy of the University of Illinois Sports Information Office.

A movie poster from Grange's brief Hollywood career. Courtesy of Wheaton College Special Collections.

Grange speaking at his Hall of Fame induction, 1963. Courtesy of Wheaton College Special Collections.

Grange visiting Memorial Stadium in 1974. Courtesy of the University of Illinois Sports Information Office.

Grange speaking to a crowd at his alma mater, renamed Wheaton Central High School, in 1974. Courtesy of Wheaton College Special Collections.

FALL 1991 · $2.9

Sports Illustrated
CLASSIC

AN
ORIGINAL
SUPERSTAR

October 18, 1924: Red Grange scores four touchdowns in twelve minutes

25 UNFORGETTABLE MOMENTS IN SPORTS

Upset! Browns beat Eagles, 1950
Could Bob Cousy play in today's NBA?

In 1991, sixty-seven years after his greatest feat, Grange was featured on the cover of a special issue of *Sports Illustrated*. Courtesy of Culver Pictures, for *Sports Illustrated;* copyright © Time, Inc.

10

Big Money Beckons—One Million Dollars' Worth

THERE WERE MANY who thought I made a big mistake when I turned pro after my last college game in the late fall of 1925. Professional football in those days was frowned upon by faculty representatives, coaches, athletic directors and the commissioner of athletics for the Big Ten Conference. It was hard to find anyone in college circles for it.

In particular, Amos Alonzo Stagg of Chicago was bitterly opposed to pro football and Fielding H. Yost of Michigan publicly admitted he had discouraged his athletes from following a professional career as a coach or player. George Huff, athletic director of Illinois, was equally vehement against pro football despite his being an ex-professional baseball player. For a time Major John L. Griffith, Big Ten commissioner, could see no harm in a college football player playing for pay, but finally was won over by Stagg and Yost.

The big objection to pro football was, I believe, the money involved. If a star player could step out after three years of intercollegiate competition and earn more money in a few months than a professor makes in an entire year, it was inevitable some people were

89

going to be unhappy. To best illustrate my point on the money angle, it is a fact that rigid rules were enforced in the conference at the time, whereby a coach or athletic director could not have a rank beyond associate professor, nor receive a salary in excess of a faculty member of that rank. This was done to avoid a jealous feeling among members of the academic staff for those in the athletic department.

I think another reason why college officials objected was their fear that pro football might take away some of the glamor of the college game and ultimately affect the gate.

Of course, time has changed all that. Today pro football occupies the same high position in the sports world as college football. Both operate under the classification of big business and neither has appreciably affected the other's attendance figures. Practically every pro-football player and coach are former big-name college football players and coaches. College players can be openly drafted by pro teams the year their class graduates. And college football coaches are generally as high-salaried as college presidents. Naturally it was impossible back in 1925 for me or anyone else, no matter how optimistic, to foresee all the changes that have taken place. Yet if I were placed in the same position today as I was then, I would still follow the identical course. I wish to make the point strong that I have never for one instant regretted what I did.

The story behind my turning professional and my association with Charlie Pyle, who was responsible for the whole thing, begins the second week of my senior year at Illinois. I was about to take my seat in a Champaign movie house one Saturday night when an usher approached me. Handing me a slip of paper with a few words scribbled on it he said, "Mr. Pyle who runs this theater wants you to have this. It's a pass that'll get you in the Virginia Theater as often as you want for the rest of the year. And you can use it for the Park Theater, too, since Mr. Pyle operates both places." I was very pleased with the offering not only because I liked going to the movies but since this was the first time I had ever received anything free while I was at Illinois.

Several days later I went to the Virginia again. As I entered the theater I was greeted in the lobby by Mr. Pyle and invited up to his office. I had heard his name mentioned many times before, but never met him. After exchanging a few pleasantries, he got around to the real reason for his wanting to see me.

"How would you like to make one hundred thousand dollars, or maybe even a million?" Pyle asked. I was momentarily stunned. Regaining my composure, I quickly answered the query in the affirmative. When I attempted to find out what Pyle had in mind he told me he had a plan, but wasn't at liberty to reveal the details at the time. He said he'd contact me in a few weeks and made me promise that after leaving his office I wouldn't mention our conversation to anyone.

I found out later that Pyle left the next day for Chicago to confer with George Halas and Ed Sternaman, co-owners of the Chicago Bears. He offered them a tentative deal whereby I would join their team immediately after my last college game against Ohio State. I was to play in the remaining league games that season and then go on tour with the Bears in a series of exhibition games that Pyle would book himself from Florida to the West Coast.

According to Pyle's proposition, the Bears were to share the gate receipts approximately fifty-fifty with us. This Pyle intended to split sixty-forty in my favor. At first Halas and Sternaman balked at the percentage figures, but after sparring into the wee hours of the morning, finally agreed to terms. Pyle then left Chicago to book the exhibition games in the West and Far South.

It was three weeks before I saw Pyle again. I learned then, for the first time, the full details of what he'd been up to. The arrangements he made with the Bear owners seemed agreeable to me and we shook hands on it. But he stressed one point. "Red, we'll sign nothing, nor will you receive one cent from me, until after you've played your last college game. We don't want to do anything to jeopardize your standing as a college player." And that's the way it stood until I signed an official contract with Pyle after the Ohio game some eight weeks later.

During my senior year rumors were continually circulating about the possibility of my becoming a professional. The subject of my leaving Illinois at the end of the collegiate football season became a topic for national discussion. Talk had it that a group of eastern sport magnates headed by Charles Stoneham of the New York Giants and Jake Ruppert of the New York Yankees baseball teams were planning to organize pro-football teams and that I was being sought as one of the key players. There was further talk about my touring with the famous Four Horsemen of Notre Dame. All this was mere hearsay. No one other than Pyle ever approached me while I was at Illinois and we kept our plans with Halas and Sternaman secret until after the Ohio State game.

One week before the battle in Columbus, the *Champaign News-Gazette* called me into their office and practically accused me of having signed a contract to play pro ball. They told me I wasn't eligible to play against the Buckeyes because of it. I replied that I had not affixed my signature to any contract and defied them to produce evidence to the contrary. At this point I put on my hat and walked out.

The Champaign paper obviously hoped to uncover a sensational exposé. My firm denial left them with no other choice but to drop the matter. If I had been seriously suspected of signing a contract with Pyle or anyone else to play professional football, I would have been put on the carpet long before by Major John Griffith, then commissioner of athletics for the Big Ten, or by the officials of my own university. This was never done, nor was it deemed necessary.

Two days before the Buckeye-Illinois battle there was a report that L. W. St. John, the Ohio State athletic director, might challenge my eligibility to play against his team because of the rumors that I had

93

inked a professional contract. St. John answered the report with: "If Red Grange denies the rumor, his word is good enough for me."

Down through the years many unkind remarks have been made about Charlie Pyle. Labeled "Cash-and-Carry," he was pictured as a notorious money-hungry promoter who ruthlessly exploited and used me to further his own ambitions. Nothing could be further from the truth. Pyle was always more than fair to me and one of the finest men I have ever known. It was a genuine pleasure to be associated with him. I wouldn't have missed the experience for the world.

Pyle was about forty-five when I met him. He was a shade over six feet tall and weighed about 195 pounds. He had gray hair and a neatly trimmed mustache. An immaculate dresser, his clothes were made to order by the most exclusive tailors. He always carried a cane, wore spats, a derby and a diamond stickpin in his tie. He was suave, brilliant and perhaps the greatest supersalesman of his day. Pyle came up with more ideas in one day than most men come up with in a lifetime.

A lot of hogwash has been written that almost everyone, including George Huff, Bob Zuppke, and my father, tried to discourage me from casting my lot with the pros. The plain fact is that no one except the newspapers ever brought up the subject until Zup questioned me about my future plans as we traveled on the train to Columbus for the Ohio State encounter.

Zup had refrained from saying anything earlier, although he was disturbed no end by reporters who hounded me all season. When he finally did ask me, I hedged by saying I would tell him anything he wanted to know after the game.

The contest with the Buckeyes was played on November 21st before a packed house of 85,500, the largest crowd ever assembled anywhere up to that time for a football contest. On the eve of the game I was supposed to head a big float parade. Zup, trying to spare me the excitement, arranged for one of my teammates to impersonate me. I was thus able to retire early, and the crowd never knew the difference.

In the game I carried the ball twenty-one times and passed nine times for a total of 195 yards. I wasn't able to rack up a touchdown myself, but threw a short pass to Chuck Kassel, our right end, in the second period and he went over for the tally from the seven-yard line. Toward the end of the battle I intercepted an Ohio pass and ran it back thirty-seven yards. Earl Britton scored a touchdown in the first quarter and accounted for the two points after touchdown as we defeated Ohio State 14-9.

The Buckeyes got two of their nine points on a safety when a punt got away from me and rolled over the goal in the second period. Halfback Elmer Marek, who was practically the entire Ohio offense that day, scored on a spectacular seventy-two-yard gallop in the third quarter and kicked the extra point.

As the gun went off, ending the game, reporters

swarmed about and pressed me for a statement. I announced for the first time my intention to play with the Chicago Bears and informed them I was going to sign a contract in Chicago the following day.

Zup, visibly disturbed by the news, drove with me from the stadium to the hotel. Mrs. Zuppke was along and we spent almost an hour in a cab as Zup ordered the driver to "keep driving" while he tried desperately to make me change my mind. "Keep away from professionalism and you'll be another Walter Camp," he pleaded. "Football isn't a game to play for money." My reply summed up what I believed all along. "You get paid for coaching, Zup, why should it be wrong for me to get paid for playing?"

We finally parted and I didn't see Zup again for about three weeks. By then I had played in several pro games. We were attending the annual Elks banquet in Champaign for the Illinois team and Zup was the principal speaker. During the course of his speech he berated me for joining the pro ranks. I thought his remarks were completely uncalled for. I had done my very best during the three varsity seasons I played for him and now that my college football career was over felt what I did from then on was my own affair. I was so mad at Zup at the time I got up from my place at the speaker's table and left the hall while he was still talking. The next day we had both forgotten the incident.

The Sunday immediately after the Ohio game I met Charlie Pyle in Chicago at his office in the Morrison

Hotel. There I signed the contract which made him my manager. Later that day Halas and Sternaman of the Bears came over and Pyle and I signed our pact with them. Now I was a pro.

11

Seven Games in Ten Days

WHEN I JOINED the Chicago Bears there were eighteen teams in the National Professional Football League. But there wasn't enough activity at the turnstiles to support half that number. There was such a lack of interest in the pro game that the league didn't even hold a championship play-off at the end of the season. Fans just seemed to prefer the college brand of football. And the fact that the big names in college football were against the pro game made matters worse.

Yet pro football in 1925 was good football. Many of the players were former college stars who continued to give their all to the game despite the small monetary return. The big problem was to get the newspapers to give the pro sport the publicity it so badly needed. Stories about the happenings in the professional league were usually buried on the second or third pages of the sports section. Had the same space been devoted to pro football as pro baseball, the former would probably have caught the public's fancy from the very beginning.

I made my pro debut in Chicago against the Chicago Cardinals on Thanksgiving Day, November 26, 1925.

Thanks to a tremendous barrage of publicity that accompanied my joining the pro ranks, 36,000 fans crowded into Wrigley Field to watch the game. It was the largest turnout ever recorded up to that time for a pro game.

The Cardinals had a great team. Their offensive power centered around Quarterback Paddy Driscoll, a Northwestern University immortal and one of the greatest all-around football players the game has ever known. In the kicking department particularly, Driscoll had no peers. During that 1925 season the Cardinals, playing fourteen league games, wound up with a record of eleven wins, one tie and two losses. The Bears were also strong. They had stars like George Trafton, Hunk Anderson, Ed Healey, George Halas and Jim McMillen in the line and Laurie Walquist, Joe Sternaman and Ed Sternaman in the backfield. Anderson and Trafton played their college football at Notre Dame, Healey at Dartmouth, and Halas, McMillen, Walquist and the Sternaman brothers were former Illini.

I entered the Bears-Cardinals contest under a handicap. I had only three days' practice prior to the game and didn't know too many of the Bears' signals. Coaches Halas and Sternaman employed a "T" formation and although it was vastly different from what we know today as the "T," it was still an adjustment for me to make from the single wing Zuppke used at Illinois.

I made ninety-two yards against the Red Birds that day, but wasn't able to get away for a touchdown. My longest gains came on punt returns. On defense I intercepted a Cardinal pass on our own five-yard line and, although I didn't get far with the ball, broke up the opposition's one serious scoring threat of the afternoon.

As was expected, the Bears-Cardinals clash was hard fought, and finally wound up in a 0-0 tie. The customers left the park somewhat disappointed that I was unable to scamper for a touchdown, but satisfied they saw a good football game.

On Sunday, three days after the clash with the Cardinals, we played an encore at the Cubs' ball park. This time we faced the Columbus Tigers. Thanks again to the wonderful support we got from the newspapers, 28,000 defied a snowstorm to watch us nose out the Tigers 14-13. As in the Cardinal game I was unable to cross the goal line, but succeeded in plowing 140 yards through the snow in the thirty minutes I played. I threw two completed passes, one that went to right halfback Walquist for a net gain of thirty-two yards, and a tally.

The following Wednesday, December 2nd, the Bears played an exhibition game against a hurriedly recruited eleven called the Donnelly Stars in Sportsman's Park, St. Louis. The weather was so cold only about eight thousand were on hand to witness the one-sided battle. We romped over them 39-6 and I accounted for four of the touchdowns. Earl Britton, my former teammate at Illinois, made his debut in the Bears' line-up as a fullback. He had signed with the team a few days before.

100

We boarded a train for Philadelphia immediately after the game since we were due, on Saturday, to meet the Frankfort Yellowjackets in Shibe Park. It had rained heavily in Philly the night before and the muddy playing conditions resembled the Penn-Illinois game of a few weeks back. Before forty thousand rain-soaked fans, the Bears beat the Yellowjackets 14-0. I proved to be a good mud horse again by scoring both touchdowns. The Chicago *Tribune* reported to the home-town folks: "Mud Plastered Grange Sears Jackets."

On December 6th, the next day, we took on the New York Giants in the Polo Grounds. The New York papers gave the game such a big build-up lines started forming outside the stadium in the morning. When kickoff time arrived, we had a packed house of 65,000.

At the half we were leading 12-7, thanks to two touchdown sprints by Quarterback Joe Sternaman. In those first two periods my contribution consisted of receiving a pass from Walquist for a twenty-two-yard gain and throwing a pass to him for twenty-three more.

In the third period neither team scored. But in the last quarter I intercepted a pass intended for the Giants' Lynn Bomar and ran it down the side lines thirty yards for a touchdown. The game ended with the Bears on the long end of a 19-7 victory.

The Bears took a terrific physical beating against New York. Although we had won, it was one of the most bruising battles I had ever been in. I especially remember one play when Joe Alexander, the Giants' center, almost twisted my head off in making a tackle.

It was clear we were all beginning to show the wear and tear of our crowded schedule. After that encounter with the Giants, the Bears were no longer able to field a team free of injuries.

We were due in Washington, D.C., on Tuesday to play another exhibition, but Pyle and I decided for business reasons to remain in New York an extra day. Opening up our hotel room to all callers we collected about $25,000 in certified checks for endorsements of a sweater, shoe, cap, doll and soft drink. We turned down a tie-up with a cigarette company because I didn't smoke.

We also signed a movie contract that day. Pyle then flashed a $300,000 check for the gathering reporters to see. Accordingly, newspapers around the country carried the story that I was to receive that fantastic amount for becoming an actor. They even ran a photograph of the draft. Unfortunately, the whole thing was just another one of Pyle's wild publicity stunts. In reality the check was a phony. We received only a few thousand dollars for signing the contract and the promise of about $5,000 per week while making a picture.

Instead of getting a percentage of the gate after every game, as reported, I just drew money as I went along. It was after the fracas in the Polo Grounds that Pyle presented me with my first cut, a check for fifty thousand dollars. Although it was far below what I was reputed to have earned, I didn't think it too bad for ten days' work.

In Washington's Clark Griffith Stadium we whipped

a local pickup team 19-0. I didn't do much, as I tried to save myself for the game with the Providence Steamrollers in Boston the next day. My contribution to victory was a drop-kick point after touchdown. The team we played in Washington was definitely not composed of good football players but were, for the most part, a tough bunch of sand-lot players who mauled and roughed us up at every opportunity.

While in Washington I was introduced to President Calvin Coolidge in the White House by Senator McKinley of Illinois. The President, more of a fisherman than a football fan, simply asked me where I lived and wished me luck.

Arriving in Boston on Wednesday morning, December 9th, for the game with the Steamrollers, the Bears were in a pitiful condition, with many of us bandaged from head to foot. I was in particularly bad shape. I had hurt my left arm in New York and it was still badly swollen. Andy Lotshaw, the Bears' trainer, worked feverishly all night on the train to help ease our miseries and prepare us for the next assault.

Under such conditions it was to be expected the Bears would not fare well against the Providence eleven. We lost 9-6 and the best I could do was eighteen yards on five tries. I attempted three forward passes and had one intercepted. My arm was in such pain I couldn't do anything right. Jim Crowley and Don Miller of the famous Notre Dame Four Horsemen played in the backfield for the Steamrollers.

I was booed for the first time in my football career in the Boston game. It made me aware of something

I had never thought of before—that the public's attitude toward a professional football player is quite different from the manner in which they view a college gridder. A pro's performance is evaluated much more critically and he is less likely to be forgiven when a mistake is made. A pro must deliver, or else.

It was reported I was a very dejected young man after that experience in Boston. Babe Ruth was supposed to have come into the locker room following the game to offer some sage words of advice. "Don't get too thin skinned. You've got to expect a lot of knocks in the professional racket and you've got to take a lot of criticism and a lot of insults that you didn't get before," the papers had him saying to me. The fact of the matter is I saw Ruth before the game only when we took some publicity pictures together. His personal remarks were limited to, "Hi-yah, kid. How you doing?" We then got to talking about baseball.

We were due in Pittsburgh the next day, December 10th, for an exhibition with the Pittsburgh All-Stars in the Pirates' ball park. I should never have played. My left arm was swollen to almost twice its normal size and the pain was excruciating. Before the game Alvin "Bo" McMillin, the one-time All-American from Centre College, who gained further fame in later years as head football coach at Indiana University and of the Detroit Lions in the National League, dropped in to say hello in the locker room. When he saw the condition of my arm he strongly advised my sitting out the game. I should have followed his advice, but it was impossible on such short notice. Our contract with the local Pitt promoter called for my playing at least thirty minutes, as in all previous games with the Bears.

It had rained heavily the day before and when it was followed by freezing temperatures the turf on the playing field became like a ripped-up concrete road. We began the Pitt game with ten men on the field and several minutes went by before anybody realized it. The Bears, with no able-bodied men left among them, matched to see who would start.

Before the game was a few minutes old I was struck on my sore arm when I threw a block for our right halfback Johnny Mohardt. The physician for the Pittsburgh club ordered that I be taken out when it appeared a blood vessel in the arm ruptured and was causing a hemorrhage. I played no more that day. Unaware at the moment that I was severely injured, the crowd jeered as I left the field. The final score was 24-0, favor of the All-Stars.

En route to Pittsburgh from Boston we changed trains in New York. By that time the newspapers were filled with stories about my injury. In order to escape from the fans and reporters who sought to learn more about my condition, Pyle had me put on a teammate's cloth coat and flat hat when we got into the station while the other boy sported my fedora and raccoon coat.

After the Pitt debacle the Bears were scheduled to wind up the regular season by playing three more games in the next three days. The first one, an exhibition in Cleveland against an all-star team, was canceled when Pyle and the Bears' management decided it would be sure suicide to play without at least one day's rest. The promoter of the game was completely unsympathetic and sued us for breach of contract.

On Saturday I still wasn't well enough to don a uniform, but Halas and Sternaman's men kept a date with the Detroit Panthers in the motor city. Our battered Chicago eleven did nothing more than go through the motions and ended up getting whacked 21-0 before a small crowd of six thousand. The money for more than nine thousand tickets had to be refunded when it was announced I wouldn't be able to play. Jimmy Conzelman, owner-coach and right halfback of the Panthers, bemoaned the fact that he lost his one and only chance for a profitable day since he bought the team.

At Detroit I was introduced to the crowd at half time by the field announcer who blared, "The gentleman on my right is Red Grange, football's most famous player." The crowd let out with an enthusiastic cheer. Then as I walked off the field a couple of fans came down from the stands and almost yanked my good arm out of the socket.

The Bears braced themselves for their final effort against the New York Giants in Wrigley Field on Sunday, December 13th. There was a large advance ticket sale for the game, but when the Bears' team physician ruled out the possibility of my playing, the ticket booths at the Cubs' ball park remained open all day Sunday to refund money to those who wished it. Many thousands claimed refunds, but there were still over fifteen thousand in the stands at game time.

I sat on the bench during the entire contest, an unhappy witness to the Bears' fourth straight loss, 9-0. Even though I didn't get into the game, I had to be escorted out of the park to a waiting taxicab by a dozen policemen, to avoid the surging autograph seekers.

I felt badly about disappointing the fans when I had to withdraw from the Pittsburgh game and then not play at all against Detroit and New York. But I couldn't risk permanent injury. One doctor really scared me when he said the blood clot which formed in my arm as a result of the ruptured blood vessel might travel through my body and, if it reached my heart, could be fatal.

To sum up, the Bears played ten football games in seventeen days, seven of them in the short span of ten days. This was in addition to the ten games they played prior to my joining the team. It was a killing pace under any circumstances, but especially so when considering the team carried only eighteen men. Today a professional football team lists thirty-three players on its squad and plays about seventeen exhibition and league games in better than a four-month period. No other team before or since has ever attempted such a grueling schedule as the 1925 Bears—and I'm sure never will.

12
Seven-Thousand-Mile Tour

AFTER THE 9-0 licking administered by the Giants in Chicago's Wrigley Field on December 13, 1925, the Bears had eight days to relax before beginning the eight-game winter tour that Charlie Pyle had arranged. I went back to Wheaton to rest my injured arm and visit with my father and brother. For the first time in my life I had money and got a big kick out of being able to afford certain luxuries for my family. For Christmas I bought a roadster for Garland and presented Dad with a check for one thousand dollars. A few weeks earlier I paid the five hundred dollars that was due on the raccoon coat I got for myself shortly before leaving the Illinois campus.

On Monday, December 21st, I left Chicago with a greatly strengthened Bears team for Coral Gables, Florida, where we were due to open our exhibition schedule on Christmas Day. Before leaving for the South, Halas and Sternaman made some player replacements and raised the number of the squad from eighteen to twenty-two men. Some of our new team members were Paul Goebel, end; Roy Lyman, tackle; Richard Vick, quarterback; Harold Erickson, halfback; and Ralph Claypool, center. Vick had played with the

Detroit Panthers that fall and Erickson and Claypool saw service with the Chicago Cardinals. Goebel was a former All-American at Michigan.

When we arrived in Coral Gables, two days before the game, we found the town in the midst of a big land boom. Almost everyone I met was a real-estate agent. Lots changed hands two or three times a day and money seemed to be as plentiful as the water in the nearby ocean.

Pyle, Halas and Sternaman were unhappy upon discovering that the site of our initial gridiron venture in the southland was just a big, open sand field. Their concern soon changed to absolute amazement when an army of carpenters, working twenty-four hours around the clock, erected a 25,000-seat stadium in time for the contest. With tickets ranging in price from $5.50 to $18.00, the local promoter figured, despite our $25,000 guarantee, to make a killing. He was very definitely overoptimistic, for even in inflated Coral Gables the fast money boys considered the prices exorbitant and only 8,000 tickets were sold.

Getting back to the game, we won 7-0 against an All-Star team led by Tim Callahan, former All-American center from Yale. With my sore left wing nearly healed, I made ninety-eight yards in nine tries and scored the only touchdown. The day afterward the newly-built stadium was torn down.

From Coral Gables we took a short train ride to Tampa, then spent the next four days basking in the Florida sun. On New Year's Day we played the Tampa Cardinals whose line-up included Jim Thorpe and five other Carlisle University luminaries. Thorpe was about forty-one years old at that time and hadn't played much in the past several years, but it was thought to be a good publicity stunt to bring him down to Tampa for this contest. Pathetically out of shape, the once-fabulous Indian athlete fumbled several times and had a terrible time trying to move around with his old time speed.

Early in the fourth quarter I broke a 3-3 tie with the Tampa eleven by running seventy yards down the sidelines for a score. The Bears went on to make another tally and we ended up notching a 17-3 win.

The next Saturday, January 2nd, we met the Jacksonville All-Stars in Jacksonville and earned a 19-6 victory. The opposition was captained by Ernie Nevers, the brilliant All-American fullback from Stanford. Making his professional debut, Nevers was the outstanding performer of the game both on defense and offense. He intercepted two Bear passes and rolled up consistent yardage as a ball carrier. Twice he stopped me when it appeared I was about to break into the clear for a long run. My lone contribution to victory was a thirty-yard pass to our right end, Verne Mullen, for a touchdown.

We had another long layoff before our next game in New Orleans. This time it was almost a week. The players lapped up some more sunshine and gorged themselves with shrimp. On Sunday, January 10th, we played and defeated Captain Lester Lautenschlager, formerly of Tulane, and his All-Southern eleven, 14-0. I gained 136 yards in sixteen plays and scored one of

110

the touchdowns. My longest run of the contest, a 51-yard punt return, was called back for offensive holding.

From New Orleans we traveled over 1,800 miles by rail to Los Angeles where the following Saturday we played the Los Angeles Tigers in the Coliseum. A crowd of 75,000 turned out. It was said at the time to be the largest gathering ever recorded for a gridiron battle in the West.

We beat the Tigers 17-7. I scored both touchdowns and Joe Sternaman drop-kicked for the Bears' field goal. Right Halfback Roy Baker scored the lone tally for the Tigers, but George Wilson, the former Washington University All-American halfback, was easily the star of the game as he carried the ball twenty-six times and stacked up 123 yards for the Californians.

The next day, Sunday, January 17th, the Bears played in a San Diego high-school stadium against a local outfit called the California All-Stars, and we won 14-0. I was listless throughout most of the game—until late in the last quarter when I broke away for a touchdown.

While in Los Angeles I learned much to my surprise that a street in nearby Glendale had been named after me. The city council of Glendale discovered one day the town had an unnamed street, and when one of the council members, who was a football fan, suggested they call it "Grange Street," the choice was unanimously approved.

A week later, January 24th, the Bears met the San Francisco Tigers in Frisco's Kezar Stadium. The Tigers, a makeshift team assembled a couple of weeks before, were captained again by George Wilson. This time we were unable to break through their tight defense, and bowed 14-7 before 25,000 frenzied partisans. Wilson was the standout for the victors until he injured his head early in the final period and had to be taken out.

On Saturday, January 30th, we played in Portland, Oregon, against another team led by George Wilson called the Longshoremen. Still smarting from our only defeat thus far of the winter tour, the Bears won by a rout 60-3. I scored two touchdowns, one in the first period on a fifteen-yard pass from Walquist, and one in the second quarter on a forty-five-yard run. Just before the end of the second period I was badly shaken up in a pile-up and didn't get back into the game for the entire second half.

The day following we ended our tour in Seattle, Washington, by beating the Washington All-Stars 34-0. With Wilson at the helm once more, the team was composed of many of the same players we faced in Portland. Again I played only the first half, but got loose for two touchdowns and gained ninety-nine yards in nine attempts.

I received my second $50,000 check from Pyle immediately after the game in Seattle. Counting the money I drew weekly, I had earned nearly $125,000 in my first season as a professional football player. Charlie had kept his word. Now I thought I could go on to make it a million.

The Bears' eight-game exhibition series wasn't

nearly as hard on any of us physically as the ten-game schedule that followed my joining the team on Thanksgiving Day. I found it no strain to play a minimum of thirty minutes in every one of the games on the winter trip. What made the difference was the fact that we had five and a half weeks in which to play the eight tilts, besides having four more teammates to share the load. Nevertheless, we were all in need of a good long vacation. The Bears had played a total of twenty-eight games from the start of their season early in September, 1925, and I had appeared in twenty-four contests counting the eight games of my senior year at Illinois.

When I became a member of the Chicago Bears it was considered a move of such importance in the sports world, many of the outstanding sports writers of the day like Westbrook Pegler, Ford Frick and Damon Runyon were assigned by their syndicates and papers to travel with the team. They wrote about anything and everything that happened to me. Because of the reams of copy given over to me and the tremendous public interest it stirred up, the Bears were able to attract over 360,000 fans in eighteen games from Thanksgiving Day, 1925, to January 31, 1926. More than 150,000 of this impressive total was recorded on the exhibition junket that started Christmas Day. We covered one end of the country to the other, making in excess of 7,000 miles in the swing from Coral Gables to Seattle and back to Chicago again. We made enough pro-football converts all over the land to give the sport the shot in the arm it so badly needed and, from the 1925 season on, professional football began to grow steadily in popularity.

13

Pyle's Rival League

AS THE SEASON OF 1926 approached, Charlie Pyle pressed George Halas and Ed Sternaman for an interest in the Chicago Bears. He brought up the record-breaking attendance figures of the previous year and argued that the only chance the Bear owners had to continue prospering at the box office were if I remained with their Chicago club. When they turned Pyle down, he asked the National Football League for a franchise to operate a new team out of New York. He figured to build the eastern property around me and call it the New York Yankees. Unfortunately, the League moguls were unable to grant the promoter's request when Tim Mara, owner of the New York Giants football organization, refused to relinquish his territorial rights in New York.

The enterprising Pyle then decided to set up a brand new football league of his own in competition with the National Football League. He hired "Big Bill" Edwards, the former Princeton All-American, to be president at $25,000 per year, and named the newly born circuit the American Professional Football League. It was composed of the following nine teams: the Chicago Bulls; the Rock Island Independents; the

Cleveland Panthers; the Brooklyn Horsemen; the Boston Bulldogs; the Newark Bears; the Philadelphia Quakers; the Los Angeles Wildcats and the New York Yankees. The Wildcats were to be the traveling club. Pyle had a controlling interest in the League, part interest with George Wilson in the Wildcats and a fifty-fifty interest with me in the Yankees. Arrangements were made with Ed Barrow of the New York Yankees baseball team to lease their new 65,000-seat stadium for all our home games.

Our Yankee football squad was made up of some outstanding former college players. Coached by Ralph Scott, former All-American from Wisconsin, we had such big names as Pooley Hubert, All-American halfback at Alabama, Wes Fry, All-American fullback at Iowa, and Eddie Tyron, former All-American halfback at Colgate and the East's greatest scorer.

The Yankees opened the season on Sunday, September 26, 1926, against the Cleveland Panthers in Cleveland's Luna Park Bowl. We attracted a gate of 22,000, the largest crowd ever assembled in Cleveland for a football game. We lost the opener to the Panthers 10-0, and my best effort of the day was a twenty-one-yard runback of a punt late in the second quarter. The fact that we didn't have sufficient time to practice before our initial appearance resulted in the team lacking the co-ordination needed to produce a winning combination.

In the next three weeks the Yankees played four games in Rock Island, Boston, Hartford and Chicago, winning all but one of the battles. We whipped the

Rock Island Independents 26-0, the Boston Bulldogs 13-0 and the New Britain All-Stars, in an exhibition contest, 19-0 before succumbing 14-0 to the Chicago Bulls in Comiskey Park. Halfback Johnny Mohardt, one-time Notre Dame star, scored both touchdowns for the Bulls and Joe Sternaman, late of the Chicago Bears, kicked the field goal. In those four tilts I crossed the goal line four times, but still wasn't playing my best football. Eddie Tyron provided our greatest strength on offense.

On Saturday, October 16th, the day before our game with the Bulls, I went down to Champaign to catch a glimpse of some of my old teammates in action. It was great fun assuming the role of a spectator and cheering Illinois on to a 13-6 victory over the Iowa Hawkeyes. When someone spotted me in the stands I was asked over the loudspeaker system to stand up and wave to the crowd. This was the first time I had been back in Memorial Stadium since leaving the campus the previous fall.

The Yankees drew small crowds in Rock Island, Boston and Hartford. This was due in part to those cities not being large enough to support major-league football and everyone wanting to stay at home near their radios to listen to the World Series baseball games between the St. Louis Cardinals and the New York Yankees. That was the memorable 1926 series in which the Cardinals bested the Yanks in seven games with the aid of the then forty-year-old "Ol' Pete" Alexander's two masterful pitching victories and his breathtaking relief job in the final contest.

With the World Series ending in New York on Sunday afternoon, October 10th, Charlie Pyle launched an ambitious professional tennis tour in Madison Square Garden that night. Not content with merely founding a new pro-football league, Pyle had talked Suzanne Lenglen and Vincent Richards, two of the world's most famous amateur tennis players, into touring the United States and Japan for a fancy price. In August of that year, Pyle went to France himself to sign Mademoiselle Lenglen to a contract, and then brought the French star and her mother back to the States on the U.S.S. *Leviathan*.

Paul Feret, Harvey Snodgrass, Howard Kinsey and Mary Browne, four other former top-ranking amateur tennis players, completed the pro troop which toured the country for nearly four months. In the middle of February, 1927, when Richards took suddenly ill with yellow jaundice and Suzanne Lenglen asked for more money, Pyle was forced to permanently disband his new sports attraction. In spite of Mademoiselle Lenglen's demands, she was reputed to have made $100,000 up to that time, while Pyle split about half that amount with Bill Pickens, his Eastern associate in the venture. All reports to the contrary, I didn't have a thing to do with that tennis tour, financially or otherwise. My job was to play football and, as far as I was concerned, that was enough to worry about.

On Sunday, October 24th, we played our first home game of the season in New York's Yankee Stadium. Before twenty thousand onlookers we eked out a 6-0 win over George Wilson's Wildcats when Eddie Tyron

117

got away for a spectacular eighty-yard touchdown gallop in the second half. A week later we were forced to cancel a game with the Newark Bears when a torrential downpour flooded the playing field and raised havoc with New York's transportation system.

During the two-week period immediately following the washout with Newark, the Yankees and I got hot and made it four straight on our home grounds. We whipped Rock Island 35-0, Brooklyn 21-13, and Boston 24-0. In the Rock Island tilt I tallied only once, but against Brooklyn and Boston experienced my two best days of the season when I rolled up a total of thirty-three points with five touchdowns and three conversions.

By the end of October, 1926, Pyle's new football league began having its troubles. With the exception of Chicago, Philadelphia, New York and the traveling Wildcats, most of the clubs in the circuit were losing heavily. At this stage in the season Cleveland and Newark were forced to withdraw from the league for lack of sufficient funds. Several weeks later the Brooklyn team under the leadership of Harry Stuhldreher, one of the Four Horsemen of Notre Dame, left our ranks and merged with the weak Brooklyn Lions of the National Football League. Earl Britton, my former teammate at Illinois and with the Bears, automatically went along with Stuhldreher, since he was the regular fullback with the Brooklyn Horsemen.

The new Brooklyn combination played their first game in the senior loop on November 21st, and were shut out 20-0 by the Los Angeles Californians. On the

118

same Sunday, one week after we had soundly trounced Boston, the Yankees' fortunes took a sudden turn. We got beaten by the Wildcats in Yankee Stadium 16-6, and I had to leave the game near the end of the first half with a badly bruised left side.

Four days later, on Thanksgiving Day, we suffered our second setback in a row with a 13-10 loss to the Philadelphia Quakers in Yankee Stadium. I was forced to retire in the third period when the hip injury I received in the encounter with the Wildcats was severely aggravated. With just one day of rest the Yankees and Quakers met again on Saturday with almost identical results. Playing in Philadelphia's Shibe Park, we lost 13-6 while I sat out the entire game nursing my bruises. Before the second contest with the Philly eleven the Yankees stood a good chance to win the league championship, but the Quakers' two victories clinched it for themselves. Philadelphia had not played as many games as our New York team, but their won-and-lost record was considerably better.

With a record of three losses in a row, the Yankees went back to New York the very next day to face the Chicago Bulls in the final home game of the season. Because of our recent poor showing and my sore hip still preventing me from playing, only 2,500 fans paid their way into the huge Yankee Stadium to watch us get back in the win column with a 7-0 conquest of the Bulls. Eddie Tyron provided the margin of victory by scoring all the Yankee points. After the battle, Tim Mara of the football Giants, who by then was getting used to the idea of having two teams in New York, challenged the Yankees to a game in either the Polo Grounds or Yankee Stadium on Sunday, December 12th. Pyle couldn't accept the tempting offer due to a previous commitment to play the Bulls in Chicago on that date. If a Giant-Yankee game had been arranged, it certainly would have attracted a huge gate.

We beat the Bulls 7-3 on a field of mud, ice and water in Comiskey Park. It was our second win in three contests with the Bulls. I played the first half and part of the fourth quarter, but with my bruised hip still bothering me and the footing on the field treacherous, I couldn't do much. I crossed the goal line once in the first period only to have the play called back for holding in the line. Our game-winning touchdown was supplied by Halfback Larry Marks, formerly of Indiana University. Despite the fog and slush that prevailed in Chicago, we pulled 8,000 fans to the game. Across town at Wrigley Field, seven thousand bought their way into the park to see a National League game between the Chicago Bears and Pottsville which ended up in a 9-7 victory for the Bears. This should give some idea of how professional football was catching on with the fans in the Windy City and how the two rival leagues were battling it out for patronage.

The Yankees ended their first year of regular season play with only average artistic and financial success. We played a total of fourteen games and suffered five losses, winding up in second place in the league standings. In seven games at Yankee Stadium we drew about

120

116,000, while attracting in the neighborhood of 100,-000 in seven games on the road.

Within a week after finishing off the Bulls in Chicago, the Yankees took to the road again on a ten-game winter exhibition trip. We toured the towns of Texas and California with a team organized by George Wilson and called Wilson's Wildcats. The injury to my side was sufficiently healed so that I was able to play in all of the games. About the only memorable part of the tour was the night in Dallas, Texas, when several of the players and I were arrested and fined ten dollars apiece for allegedly disturbing the peace. All we did was walk into a night spot that a policeman recommended as a place for laughs. To this day I'm trying to figure that one out.

14

Hollywood Bound

I WENT TO Hollywood to make my first movie in June, 1926. That was the summer after my initial season of professional football. Before I left for the coast I took a much-needed four-month rest in Wheaton. I had great fun puttering around the three-story house I bought for Dad, Garland and myself several months earlier. We remodeled the outside with stucco and had Marshall Field & Company completely furnish the interior. The den on the third floor was like a private club. It had wood-paneled walls, leather couches and chairs, a pool table, poker tables and a bar. Dad particularly enjoyed entertaining his cronies up there. I also built a four-car garage on the lot next door and equipped it with a grease pit, gasoline pump, compression air pump, automatic tire gauge and every imaginable automotive tool. Since we had four cars between the three of us, we made good use of the garage's facilities. There was nothing I relished more than getting into some old clothes and working on the family cars.

Charlie Pyle set out for Hollywood several weeks before me in order to make all the necessary arrangements prior to my arrival. When I joined him I found he had spared few expenses to make our stay in the film capital as comfortable as possible. He rented two luxurious suites in the Ambassador Hotel, one for our living quarters, the other for an office. With Charlie everything had to be done on a grandiose scale. Beans DeWolf, my boyhood chum from Wheaton, was the third member of our party. He acted as our traveling secretary and business manager.

Bill Pickens, a successful sports promoter and friend of Pyle's, was a resident of Hollywood when we were there, and since he knew almost everyone worth knowing in the town, was very helpful in introducing us around. Shortly after I arrived, Pickens took me over to meet Jim Jeffries, the former heavyweight boxing champ. Big Jim had a home in nearby Burbank and was very proud of his vegetable garden. When I showed some interest in what seemed like an onion patch, Jim smiled and said, "Go ahead, pick some, take 'em back to the hotel with you." I did. The next morning our suite almost had to be fumigated. It turned out the onions were not really onions, but garlic. Pyle, Pickens and Jeffries ribbed me about that for days.

Sometime later I happened to drop in to an exclusive haberdashery shop which was owned partly by Douglas Fairbanks, Sr. Doug was in the store at the time and offered to match me double or nothing for a tweed suit I picked out. When I won, Fairbanks wrote on the inside label, "This suit is on you, but it's on me." I proudly kept that suit for nearly fifteen years.

When I reported for work at the old FBO Studios, now known as RKO, Ed King, the head man in charge of production, really put out the welcome mat. After I was assigned to a comfortable dressing room, he took me on a personally conducted tour of the lot. Except for King and the other studio officials at FBO, no one else in Hollywood paid much attention to me. Several big names from the athletic world had already appeared in films, but failed to make much of an impression on the movie-going public. There were many who did not expect me to fare any better.

The film the studio had set for me was a rah-rah college story entitled *One Minute To Play*. The plot dealt with the adventures of a youth whose football record at high school was considerably better than his class marks. When he finished high school his father sent him off to college—only after he agreed not to play football there. Due to a mix-up that took place on the train, the young man ended up at the wrong school and subsequently broke his promise to his father about playing football. Right before the crucial game of the season the father discovered his son's deception and descended upon the scene raising havoc with all concerned in an attempt to keep the boy from further participating in the sport. However, he finally relented. In the closing minutes of play in the big game Red Wade, the young hero of the yarn, is allowed to get back into uniform and singlehandedly clinches a victory for his Alma Mater. Of the dramatic finale to the picture Mae Tinee, the movie critic of the Chicago *Tribune,* had this to say: "The picture ends with an honest-to-goodness game that is considerable of a sensation." As I portrayed the role of Red Wade, Miss Tinee went on: "If you've never seen Red Grange play football, now's your chance, for he plays it like everything in this picture."

Others in the film were Charles Ogle as Mr. Wade and Edythe Chapman as Red Wade's mother. Mary McAllister was cast as Sally Rogers, young Wade's girl friend, Lee Shumway as the football coach, Jay Hunt as Mr. Todd, the college prexy, and football star George Wilson as the key player on the opposing team. The screenplay for *One Minute To Play,* written by Byron Morgan, was later novelized by Harold Sherman and won favorable acceptance by the reading public. The movie itself turned out to be surprisingly good and did a brisk business at the box office.

The football sequences of *One Minute To Play* were shot in the middle of July with the temperatures in the high nineties. For the crowd scenes at the game the producer needed a large number of people. Ordinarily he could count on a good turnout to watch the filming of the picture and thus eliminate the necessity of hiring thousands of extras, but due to the hot weather, those in attendance would certainly be clad in shirt sleeves, straw hats and blouses. Since the game was supposed to be played in the Midwest on a fall afternoon, the crowd couldn't be shown in such attire. Charlie Pyle came up with the solution to the problem. He induced the studio to put an advertisement in one of the Los Angeles papers that George Wilson's team would play Red Grange's team in a regulation

125

game, and admission was free to anyone who came dressed in fall apparel. The results of Pyle's brainstorm were unbelievable. Fifteen thousand die-hard football fans turned out in felt hats, scarves, coats and jackets, and when seen on the screen couldn't be distinguished from a crowd on a chilly fall day in Ohio or Illinois.

The people at FBO were all very considerate and co-operative. Our director, Sam Wood, and script writer, Byron Morgan, were especially helpful. Wood and Morgan teamed up to do many of the early screen successes which starred such big names as Gloria Swanson and Wallace Reid. I became particularly fond of Sam Wood and often thought he would have made a great football coach because he could get a lot out of you the easy way. During my first summer in Hollywood I rarely did anything but work. The only relaxation I had was when Director Wood let me off early a few afternoons to watch the Los Angeles Angels play ball.

Making *One Minute To Play* was the worst drudgery I'd ever experienced. It took us a little better than four weeks of actual shooting time to complete the movie. To do the football sequences I spent ten straight scorching hot days in front of the cameras from dawn to sundown in full football regalia. By the time I got back to the hotel at night I cared about nothing except falling into bed. I was so tired and bored that I counted the days until the film was completed so I could get back to Wheaton.

While working in the picture I had no idea how it was turning out. I performed my job every day without keeping an account of the story line. Although I was shown a few of the rushes, I didn't see the finished product until it premiered at Chicago's Rialto Theatre on October 4, 1926, some three months later. The Rialto was a top movie-vaudeville house in those days, and I appeared in person on the stage for four shows in place of the regularly scheduled acts the first day the film played there. I arranged to be in Chicago for that engagement between Yankee football games in Cleveland and Rock Island.

Shortly after I returned home from Hollywood after completing *One Minute To Play,* I had a pretty good indication of how the picture turned out. I received several congratulatory wires from the top studio brass telling me how pleased they were with my work and that in their opinion the film was one of the best they had ever produced. After the movie was released in the fall, Mr. Joseph P. Kennedy, who had a controlling interest in FBO, tried to talk me into giving up football to devote full time to making movies for his company. I refused his flattering offer on the grounds that I considered myself a football player by profession and not an actor. Besides, I still had a contract to play another year of football for Charlie Pyle and had no intention of running out on him. Mr. Kennedy was disappointed in my decision, but did not press me further.

I went back to Hollywood to make my next picture the summer of 1927. There was a world of difference in my attitude the second time I went out there as compared to my initial exposure to the film capital.

127

The first summer I did little else besides perform my various chores at the studio and engaged in little or no contact with the film folk. But now things were different. I still worked hard to be sure, but began to get into the swing of Hollywood's social whirl. And I loved every minute of it.

In addition to Pyle, DeWolf and myself, Ralph Scott, our Yankee football coach, came out to the coast with us that year. Instead of going back to the hotel we rented an elegant ten-room house on fashionable Gramercy Place—replete with houseboy and cook. One day Scott, in a fit of anger, fired both of them. Pyle didn't appreciate the fact we were left without a cook. He ordered; "Ralph, since you took it upon yourself to let the cook go, you can have his job!" Instead of resenting the edict, Scott took up his new responsibilities with delight and remained on the job the rest of the time we were there. His cooking was a revelation, worthy of any gourmet's palate. We found out later that our Yankee football-mentor-turned-chef, had learned his art during his ranch-hand days in Montana.

We had a poker circle that met once a week which included, in addition to Pyle, Scott and myself, Walter Hires, Tom Gallery, Adolph Menjou, Lloyd Hamilton (of the movies), Al Green (a director at one of the studios), and Mark Kelly (a prominent Los Angeles sports writer). When it was our turn to play host, Ralph took time out from the game to serve some of his delicious fried chicken and special salad. The boys never stopped raving about it.

128

Every Sunday night Tom Gallery and his wife, film comedienne Zazu Pitts, held a big shindig at their home. There was so much fun to be had at those parties we never missed one. Practical jokes were always the order of the day and before the summer was over just about everyone in the crowd was a victim of some prank. We pulled a gag on Scott one night that was a lulu. Gallery had a big new radio that practically extended the width of one of the walls in his living room. What Scott didn't know was that this electronic monster was also wired to a microphone upstairs and Gallery could cut in at any time with his own personal broadcast. One night while we were sitting around listening to a sports broadcast, another voice interrupted with a special news flash. The announcement said that five thousand students at the University of Wisconsin had signed a petition asking that Ralph Scott be named coach of their school's football team. Big Ralph was almost overcome with emotion upon hearing this news. He had been an All-American at Wisconsin and always dreamed of returning to his alma mater as head football coach.

"How'd you ever do it, Scotty?" he was asked.

"Oh, I just pulled a few strings," he beamed.

"How much money you going to get?" he was further questioned.

"Oh, about six or seven thousand," came the reply.

Even though that amount was thought to be a high figure for a college coach in those days, Ralph was urged to hold out for more. "Don't take less than ten thousand," we advised him.

By this time Scotty was worked up to a high pitch. He even went so far as to start diagraming some of the plays he would use the next season. By this time we didn't have the heart to carry the joke any further. We told him the whole thing was a hoax and that the voice he heard over the radio was really Tom Gallery in the upstairs room. Scott usually had a good sense of humor, but he was so crushed in this instance he didn't know whether to laugh or cry.

The producers of my second Hollywood film decided to forego football in favor of building a story around racing. Morgan and Wood had had considerable success with automobile-racing pictures before. For me, it was a happy decision as I welcomed the chance to do something else in the off season besides play football. Also, I always had a yen to drive racing cars, and there was ample opportunity to satisfy that ambition during the filming of that picture.

Entitled *Racing Romeo,* my new movie was made mostly on location at the fairgrounds at Ventura, about fifty miles north of Hollywood. The supporting players included Walter Hires, a favorite comedian of the time, and Jobyna Ralston, who had appeared as a leading lady in many of Harold Lloyd's early films. Also in the cast were Cliff Bergere, Freddie Frame, Babe Stapp and Lou Moore, four of the country's leading race drivers. Bergere was our stunt driver.

The plot *Racing Romeo* called for Hires and me to be cast as co-owners in the garage business. We had a tough time making ends meet, and our only salvation was to snag the prize money in the Big Race that was coming up. We took an old battered racing car and patched it up with the idea of entering it in the race. When finished, it wasn't much to look at, but under the hood we had built a super power plant. The race was a combination road and track affair. The course, for the most part, was along the countryside and ended up on the track. As the hero of the yarn, I sped through haystacks, across ditches, under low bridges and encountered just about every kind of hazardous obstacle imaginable. I finally emerged the winner in an exciting neck-and-neck battle to the finish.

I wanted to do my own stunt driving, but Sam Wood insisted Cliff Bergere do the dangerous bits. He didn't want to risk the chance of my getting hurt. However, I drove in all the close-up shots. We had some of the fastest cars in the country on hand for *Racing Romeo* and I got a terrific kick out of getting behind the wheel of those souped-up jobs. I often remained at the track hours after everyone went home in order to take some extra turns on my own.

One of the people I got to know pretty well in connection with that picture was Barney Oldfield, one of the country's greatest all-time race drivers and auto pioneers. Bill Pickens, who was once Oldfield's manager, told me of the time a young, ambitious auto mechanic approached Barney and begged him to accept half-interest in his new auto-building shop in return for the use of Barney Oldfield's famous name on his cars. Oldfield was much too busy at the time to become involved in any business venture and reportedly passed up the offer. The determined mechanic went ahead without Oldfield and used his own name on his horseless carriages—Henry Ford.

The Racing Romeo took a little over five weeks to make and, like *One Minute To Play,* was a silent picture. Although I never got to see the finished product, I figured it had all the earmarks of being as good a film as my first one. Unfortunately however, *The Racing Romeo* did not do well at the box office. This may have been due in part to the fact that the studio did not promote it in the grand manner that they did my previous movie. Possibly the wrangling which developed between Charlie Pyle and the studio heads over money matters, and my refusal to devote full time to picturemaking, caused them to lose interest in me. In any event, it made little difference to me then. Football was my only real concern anyway.

15

My Luck Gives Out

THE FUTURE LOOKED bright for Charlie Pyle and me at the start of the 1927 football season. Charlie had made peace with the National Professional Football League. He agreed to disband his rebel American League in exchange for a National League franchise for our New York Yankees. If I could only continue as a big gate attraction for a few more seasons, until the Yankees as a team developed a loyal band of followers, we were certain to wind up as co-owners of very valuable football property. I didn't think I'd have much to worry about when my playing days were over. But, as I sadly discovered, fate has a strange way of changing one's plans.

The Yankees opened the 1927 season in Dayton against the Dayton Triangles with a 6-3 victory. One week later, before twenty thousand in the University of Detroit's stadium, we whipped the Cleveland Bulldogs 13-7. The Bulldogs were captained by Benny Friedman, the former Michigan ace, who had made his pro debut against the New York Giants one week earlier. Neither Friedman nor I did any scoring, but my former Big Ten rival showed well as a pro quarterback. He tossed four passes good for a total of forty yards, and in the third period intercepted a Yankee pass that should have gone for a touchdown.

With two straight victories under our belts we prepared to face the powerful Chicago Bears in Wrigley Field on Sunday, October 16th. A capacity crowd of thirty thousand turned out, which was the largest gathering for a professional football contest in Chicago since I bowed there as a pro two years before. Immediately prior to the game there were riots at the park as thousands of fans, unable to gain admittance, stormed the center-field bleacher gates, climbed the fences and swarmed the side lines. Others rushed into the grandstands on the south end of the field, which had been boarded off for alterations. It literally broke Pyle's heart to see all those people get in free.

We lost to the Bears 12-0, although I had one of the best days of my pro career. I averaged five yards per try, including runs of twenty and twenty-five yards, threw the only completed Yankee pass and intercepted one of Paddy Driscoll's long heaves. In the second quarter I nailed Driscoll on the eleven-yard line after the Bear quarterback ran a Yankee kickoff back eighty-four yards through our entire team. In the final half minute of play, Eddie Tyron faded back to toss me a pass in a desperate, last-ditch effort to score. As I reached up high for the ball, I collided with Center George Trafton of the Bears. My cleats got caught in the ground as I fell, and when Trafton accidentally toppled on me I twisted my right knee. I felt an excruciating pain in the knee and was unable to get up. As I lay on the ground the crowd cheered words of encouragement. Hundreds formed lines around me a few minutes later when I was hurried into the dressing room. No one knew it then, but they had seen the Galloping Ghost gallop for the last time.

This was the fourth time in almost ten years of organized football that I was seriously injured. I had been cracked in the head at Toledo while playing my final season at Wheaton High, got my shoulder banged up against Minnesota my junior year at Illinois, suffered a badly bruised arm my first season of pro ball with the Bears, yet survived these injuries to come back stronger than ever. But now, with my leg involved, it was a different matter—for a football player depends more upon his legs than any other part of his body. They are his greatest single asset. When the power and maneuverability of a player's legs are destroyed, he loses forever his effectiveness. Such was the case with me.

My injury was diagnosed as a torn tendon. Then, when the knee started to swell, it was suspected that water had formed on it as a complication. I couldn't stand on my right limb nor bend it without severe pain. Numerous specialists examined me, but none agreed on what to prescribe. Some advised surgery, some rest, others diathermy treatments. I followed the latter treatment and it seemed to help a little. However, I hobbled around for the next four weeks on crutches, still in misery when I put weight on the leg. During that period I appeared in uniform at all the Yankee games, but limited my activity to being introduced at half time. With all this I was confident the injured leg would respond to treatment and I would be ready to return to action before too long.

The attendance at Yankee games fell off badly after my injury, and Pyle and I became deeply concerned about it. To make it worse, I was bound by contract with the other teams in the National League to play in all Yankee games as long as I was in one piece. With such pressure on me I forced myself to return to the football wars against the Chicago Cardinals in Yankee Stadium on November 13th, just four weeks after that fateful day in Chicago.

Shifting from left halfback to quarterback so I wouldn't be called upon to do much running, I was just a shell of my former self in that Cardinal game. The Yankees won 20-6 that day, in spite of me. Eddie Tyron was the star of the game. The Yankee stalwart scored twice and was all over the field. Even though we won by a comfortable margin, it was a tough battle. Our right halfback, Roy "Bullet" Baker, the former Southern California star, suffered four broken ribs and two fractures in his left hand and was lost to us for the remainder of the season. In reporting the game *The New York Times* wrote:

> It was a gallant effort by the former Illinois flash and it was roundly applauded. However, Grange could not limp fast enough to cover passes and could not back up the line with efficiency. He did carry the ball and he did catch a pass and also threw others. But each time there were a lot of

people holding their breath lest that very obviously bandaged leg give way.

I should never have returned to action as soon as I did. As careful as I tried to be, the injury to the knee was aggravated in that Cardinal battle and the next day a plaster cast was put on my leg from the middle of the thigh halfway down the calf. The doctor warned that the cast might have to remain on for some time. Disregarding the doctor's orders, Pyle and I agreed to announce to the press that I would be ready to play a full sixty minutes against Benny Friedman's Cleveland Bulldogs on Thanksgiving Day, just eleven days hence. Since our team wasn't drawing much at the gate without me, it was decided to cancel an exhibition contest scheduled the Sunday between the Cardinal and Bulldog games.

Against Cleveland on November 24th we lost 30-19 before twenty thousand onlookers in Yankee Stadium. As promised, I played most of the game. It was the first Yankee defeat of the season on our home grounds. Playing at quarterback again I didn't do any running, but got off a few completed forward passes for short gains. However, I might just as well have remained on the sidelines since I didn't contribute much to our team's over-all offense or defense. I was in bad shape and I knew it, but I couldn't give up. No one in the stands that day knew I left my cane in the dressing room before coming out on the field.

Three days after our loss to Cleveland, the Yankees were beaten again in Providence by the Providence

Steamrollers. This time it was by a 14-7 margin. I played the entire first half. Although I didn't carry the ball, I threw six passes, completing four for gains aggregating seventy-five yards, and caught two Tyron passes good for a total of forty-three yards. Incidentally, on the same date the New York Giants, by beating the Chicago Bears in Chicago 13-7, won the pro title.

On December 4th we battled the Giants at the Polo Grounds and lost our third straight 14-0 on a snow-sprinkled gridiron. I played the entire game although still severely handicapped and in much pain. On occasion I seemed to flash my old form, but when the going got rough my knee wouldn't hold up. As long as I ran in a straight line it wasn't too bad, but when I attempted to cut, the knee folded under me. Hinkie Haines, the Giants' quarterback, provided the fans with the thrills in the opening quarter when he ran a Yankee kick seventy-five yards for a touchdown. *The New York Times* headline in the sports pages the next day read: "10,000 See Giants Beat Yankee Eleven, 14-0, Despite Grange's Brilliant Play." The story under that headline said in part:

Grange, although severely handicapped with a crippled right leg, played the entire game and he carried more than his share of the burden. He led the team, directed the aerial offensive, and his work of running back punts was reminiscent of his flashy work at Illinois, which won national prominence for him. He showed no inclination

138

to save himself and when not carrying the ball he generally took out his man and cared for any other assignment that fell to the lot of the interfering back.

We wound up our regular season the following Sunday with another game against the Giants. This time we played at Yankee Stadium, and again we lost, by practically an identical score, 13-0. I was in at quarterback for almost the full sixty minutes, and performed nearly as well as I did the previous week although I still used a cane off field. To make matters worse, late in the game my throwing hand was badly bruised. In the closing minutes of play I had to be taken out when I was severely shaken up by three Giant tacklers as I tried to skirt around the left side of the line.

Instead of retiring for the season and nursing my battered knee, I played with the Yankees through the month of January, 1928, on an exhibition tour of the Pacific coast. Pitted against various all-star teams led by George Wilson and Benny Friedman, I kept going because, at the young age of twenty-four, I refused to believe that I couldn't bounce back to my old form. I was positive I could play myself back into shape. But those additional games only served to further aggravate my condition and, when the tour was ended, it became apparent I had done irreparable damage to the knee. For the first time since I was hurt, nearly four months before, I began worrying over the possibility that I might be through as a football player.

16

A Business Partnership
Is Dissolved

THE LAST STOP on the Yankees exhibition tour
of the Pacific coast, the end of January, 1928, was Los
Angeles. As long as I was out there, I thought I'd
hang around while Charlie Pyle set the stage for his
sponsorship of the historic Transcontinental Marathon from Los Angeles to New York. I helped Charlie with a few details, then accompanied him along
the route of the marathon as far as Chicago. While
the runners tirelessly pounded the pavement, we
traveled in grand style in the $25,000 bus Pyle had
specially built for the event. One newspaperman covering the marathon appropriately referred to the cus-
tom-made vehicle, which was equipped with a radio,
shower bath, kitchen, living room and bedroom with
sleeping accommodations for six, as a "land yacht."

The longest marathon in history, Pyle's fantastic
sports extravaganza began in Los Angeles on Sunday,
March 4, 1928. Nearly every race and color were represented among the 275 entrants with ages ranging
from sixteen to sixty-three. They were after nearly
$50,000 in prize money. The winner was to get
$25,000, runner-up $10,000, $5,000 for third place,

$2,500 for fourth position and $1,000 each for the next six finishers. Additional prize money was offered for the best time between certain prescribed points along the marathon's itinerary. Charlie supposedly took in more than enough to defray all the expenses connected with the derby by selling close to half a million programs at twenty-five cents apiece. Since millions of persons watched the strange band of athletes as they passed through their towns and cities, Pyle always contended the "Bunion Derby," as the marathon was more popularly called, was the greatest free show ever offered the American public.

Seventy-one of the original 275 made it to Chicago by May 5th. And on Saturday, May 26th, fifty-five weary weather-beaten runners arrived in New York with Andrew Payne of Claremore, Oklahoma, leading the pack. John Salo of Passaic, New Jersey, staggered in a close second. Once in New York, the exhausted survivors of the 3,485-mile trek across the country were required to wind up matters with a twenty-five-mile sprint in Madison Square Garden. Pyle had hoped to lure large crowds into the garden to witness the agonizing spectacle, but only eight hundred bought tickets while thousands gaped outside.

At this juncture I wish to emphasize that like the Suzanne Lenglen – Vincent Richards tennis tour and the numerous other Pyle promotions, I had nothing whatsoever to do with the "Bunion Derby" financially or otherwise. It was entirely Pyle's baby. I was merely an interested bystander.

141

I joined Charlie Pyle in New York a few days after the excitement of the marathon's conclusion had passed. It was then that we sat down to discuss the renewal of our now expired contract. Since my football future was in doubt, due to my injured knee, I decided it unwise to continue our pact. I also elected to withdraw my interest in the New York Yankees football team. The Yankees had been losing heavily and I could no longer afford to continue pouring money into the property. I thus ended a memorable three-year association with perhaps the greatest sports impresario the world has ever known.

Pyle kept the Yankees intact during the regular 1928 season with the aid of Gibby Welch, Pittsburgh's fine All-American back. However, despite Welch's brilliant play the team had a bad year, compiling a record of four wins, one tie and eight losses, and winding up in seventh place in the league standings. The attendance at Yankee games fell off so badly Charlie fell heavily in debt and was forced to drop the club's franchise at the end of the '28 campaign.

During my extended stay in Los Angeles before tagging along with Pyle and his runners to Chicago, and later when I went to New York to talk contract with him, I continued consulting various prominent doctors about my knee. I was still hopeful of finding a cure, but received little encouragement that I would ever play football again. I was told that if I did, I might incur serious permanent injury and become crippled for life. My future looked black indeed. I didn't know quite what to do.

Back in Chicago in early June, 1928, Frank Zambreno, a motion-picture distributor in the city and a friend of Pyle's, approached me and said he thought he could negotiate a picture deal in Hollywood with Universal Pictures if I were interested. I welcomed the proposition and happily set out for the coast again for another crack at the movies when we got the okay from the studio to come out there. This time, instead of making the trip with an entire entourage, I took only my father along and we rented a modest little bungalow in Los Angeles. Dad had plenty of free time on his hands at this point, having retired two years before from duty in the sheriff's office in Wheaton. Once in Hollywood, the producer ran into story trouble and we waited around for over two months without anything happening. Finally, unable to take the inactivity any longer, I made a cash settlement for the time I had lost with Carl Laemmle Jr., the head of the studio, and returned home with Dad.

When the 1928 football season rolled around and I was unable to return to action, I felt like a duck out of water. It was the first time since I was a kid in Wheaton that I failed to don football togs in the fall of the year. I was deeply concerned about the prospect of being washed up as a player, but managed to keep my mind temporarily off my troubles by going on a six-month vaudeville tour that Frank Zambreno lined up for me. Appearing in cities like Chicago, St. Louis, Toledo, Brooklyn, New York, Boston, New Haven and Bridgeport, I did a football skit that was given the corny title, *C'mon Red*. The act was given top billing all over the circuit and I earned a nice piece of change for my efforts. In Chicago, where I was always considered a home-town boy, I worked the Oriental, Paradise, Tower, Harding and Northshore theaters, with the assistance of such well-known band leaders of the day as Paul Ash, Mark Fisher, Al Morey and Frankie Masters. The newspaper ads, in announcing my appearance at the various theaters, attempted to entice customers with this line of copy: "See Red and a big cast of entertainers in a rousing, rollicking revue packed with college spirit, syncopation and fun."

In the summer of 1929 I was back in Hollywood again. I went out there with Zambreno when he arranged for me to do a talking picture for Nate Levine who had gained considerable prominence as the "King of the Serials." Levine had worked up a neat, twelve-episode vehicle for me called *The Galloping Ghost*. Loaded with thrills and action, it was the story of a gang of shady characters who got involved in a taxicab war while making attempts to fix football games. As the hero of the film, I naturally apprehended the culprits in the end. My supporting cast included Dorothy Gulliver as the girl friend, with Stepin Fetchit and Tom Dugan supplying the comedy relief.

Every chapter of *The Galloping Ghost* was chock full of breath-taking sequences. We blew up houses, had motorcycle and speedboat chases, jumped from one plane to another in mid-air, plunged autos off cliffs, and swung from balconies and chandeliers in bruising gang fights. Doing practically all of the stunt work myself, I was black and blue from head to foot by the time the picture was completed.

Making *The Galloping Ghost* was, without doubt, the most strenuous work I have ever done in my life. What made it even more difficult was the task of learning spoken lines for the first time. Talking pictures were still new in 1929, and it was a difficult adjustment for even the most seasoned actors in Hollywood.

It took just five weeks to finish the twelve chapters of *The Galloping Ghost*—although its running time of nearly four hours was equal to the length of two regular features. To finish the picture in that short time we worked seven days a week, sometimes as much as eighteen hours a day. Levine would call for me every morning at five o'clock and we'd stop in the coffee shop near the studio for breakfast. As soon as it was light outside we were on the set ready for action. In the evenings the cast and crew moved indoors for the interior scenes. Levine had every movement of his movie so carefully planned there was never a minute wasted. The picture did exceptionally well at the box office for many years and, surprisingly enough, to this day still enjoys frequent bookings around the country via television.

In looking back upon my experiences making motion pictures and appearing briefly in vaudeville, I've always felt it represents one of the most memorable and worth-while chapters in my life. When I first reported for work in the film capital back in 1926, I was a shy, bashful, small-town boy despite the national prominence I had achieved for my football playing. Facing cameras, live audiences in the theaters, and mixing with all the stimulating people connected with show business did something for me. It gave me confidence and poise and made me feel a little bit more like a man of the world.

17

Successful Comeback Attempt

WHEN I RETURNED to Chicago from Hollywood in the late summer of 1929, I was in a quandary. I felt pretty certain in my own mind that I was through as a football player and thought that opinion was shared by just about everyone in football circles. But Frank Zambreno, the man who set up my vaudeville tour and was instrumental in my making the movie serial, insisted I give football another try. He told me he had spoken with George Halas, and the Bears' coach was sure that in spite of my bad knee I could still be of value to his team. I was dubious, but Zambreno, in whom I had great confidence, convinced me to at least discuss the matter with Halas. I finally went to see George and, much to my surprise, found him very enthusiastic about the prospect of my returning to the Bears as a player. In spite of my doubts I agreed to give it a whirl, for down deep I wanted to get back into football in the worst way. However, if Zambreno hadn't informed me of Halas' attitude, I don't think I would have ever approached him myself about a comeback.

I wasn't in uniform very long before I discovered

that I could still run fast, but my weak knee prevented me from being able to cut, weave or change my pace. I couldn't even attempt to get fancy, for, if I did, surely my knee would have gone one way and me the other. It was clear that now I was nothing more than a straight runner and as such would never again be a strong open field threat. Not willing to settle for mediocrity I began to work harder than ever on perfecting my defensive play. During the 1929 campaign, when I alternated at left halfback with Paddy Driscoll who was playing his last season of pro ball, Coach Halas usually put me in the game for pass defense when we were back in our own territory. Not getting many chances to carry the ball I recorded only two touchdowns that first year, while on defense I missed many blocks and tackles during the early part of the season as my timing was off due to the year's absence from the football wars. It wasn't until the last half of the campaign that I began to feel at home again on a football field. Offensively I had my best day of the 1929 season on October 27th against the Minneapolis Red Jackets. Although I didn't score in the Bears' 27-0 rout of the Red Jackets, I passed to my brother Garland (who was playing his first of three seasons with the Bears as an end) for one tally, and then took a pass myself from Quarterback Joe Sternaman in the end zone for the extra point. The stock market crashed the week we played Minneapolis, and I for one was thankful I was lucky enough to have a job at the time. Like millions of other Americans I had lost most of my savings as a result of Wall Street's collapse.

One of the things I'll never forget about that 1929 season was the spectacular one-man show Fullback Ernie Nevers of the Chicago Cardinals put on when we met his team in Comiskey Park on Thanksgiving Day, November 28th. The Cardinals, using the double wing back formation, walloped us 40-6 that day as the former Stanford All-American scored all of his team's points with six touchdowns and four conversions. The Bears' lone marker was made at the start of the second half when Fullback Walt Holmer passed to Garland Grange who scampered sixty yards to the goal.

Incidentally, my brother "Gardie" was one of the finest and surest pass receivers ever to play football. He was also extremely fast and could run a hundred yards in 9.8. However, at 168 pounds he was much too light for pro football as it was played in those days. Because of his lack of weight, he was handicapped on defense, but I've always maintained that if he were to be used strictly as an offensive end in the platoon system that came into football some years later, he could have been one of football's greatest stars. Though he played only two seasons at Illinois, "Gardie" is rated by Bob Zuppke along with Chuck Carney as an all-time Illinois end. My brother was an entirely different type of personality on the football field than I. While I was a quiet sort of player who could feel it inside, he could stimulate the entire team with his enthusiasm. He breathed fire and brimstone, and before a game we almost wanted to tie him up for fear he might go out on the field and kill somebody.

149

Midway through the 1929 season, I suffered the most painful injury I ever received in football. We were playing the New York Giants and halfway through the first quarter I banged my elbow on the ground as I tackled one of the Giants' runners. I immediately felt a strange sensation in my arm and thought it was broken. I couldn't lift the arm and never had anything hurt me so. I left the game, went up to the dressing room and lay down on the rubbing table. I was perspiring and breathing heavily when Dr. John Davis, the club physician, looked me over and said, "Red, your arm is out of the socket at the shoulder. We better get it back in as soon as possible. The longer it's out the harder it will be to put back in place and the more harm it will do." The next thing I knew, Andy Lotshaw, the Bear trainer, grabbed my left arm, a clubhouse attendant held my feet and Dr. Davis took my right arm, pulled it way up over my head and down, snapping it back in the socket. It was the most excruciating pain I have ever experienced in my life.

Although I was still sagging to the starboard, I was back in action against the same New York Giants two weeks later. After that injury, which I've always felt could be traced back to the damage done to my shoulder in the 1924 Minnesota game, trainer Lotshaw taped me from the elbow up to my shoulder for the next few seasons. Also, late in 1929 my knee began to bother me again so I had a special brace made up for protection. It was constructed out of elastic with two steel hinges along the sides and extended from about six inches below the knee to about six inches above it.

As a further precaution, Lotshaw would basket weave the knee with adhesive tape before putting on the brace. I wore that contraption every time I played until my retirement from football some five years later. With one shoulder taped and my knee encased in a brace, all I needed was a spear and shield and I would have looked like a knight in armor. How I was able to maneuver around on the field is still a mystery to me.

In 1930, with the retirement of Paddy Driscoll as an active player, I became the Bears's regular left halfback. By being able to play more often, I began to improve somewhat in my offensive game and by the time the season ended I had crossed the goal line six times. I think perhaps my best effort of the 1930 season was against the Portsmouth Spartans on November 30th. In that contest I scored one touchdown and passed to end Luke Johnsos for another as we beat the Spartans 14-6. Bronko Nagurski, the block-busting All-American tackle-fullback from Minnesota and one of football's all-time greats, made his pro debut that season. With the help of the Bronk's smashing power, the Bears were able to lift themselves from ninth place in the league standings in 1929 to third place in 1930. In the 1931 campaign the Bears again took third place and I racked up another six touchdowns. On October 11th I scored the Bears' lone touchdown as we beat the New York Giants 6-0, and the following week tallied three times as we made up a 7-0 half-time deficit and beat the Chicago Cardinals 26-13. Nagurski roared sixty-five yards for the Bears' other marker in the game against the Cardinals. At the end of the 1931 season I was named as the left halfback on the first all-league pro team ever picked.

My best year after my comeback was 1932 when I accounted for nine touchdowns and again won a place on the all-league team as the left halfback. I was captain of the Bears during that season, and kept that honor until my retirement. The Bears had a great team in 1932, winning the World Professional Football Championship on December 18th by beating Portsmouth, now the Detroit Lions, 9-0 in a play-off game. Due to inclement weather, the contest was played indoors on an undersized field in the Chicago Stadium before a near-capacity crowd of 11,198. I was kicked in the head and knocked out in the second quarter of that game; but upon returning to action in the final period, Nagurski shot me a short pass over the center of the line in the end zone for the score. Tiny Engebretsen, a guard, kicked the extra point and, minutes later, just before the game ended, the Bears got two more points on a Spartan safety.

John "Bull" Doehring and Bill Hewitt played their first year in pro football with the 1932 Bears. Doehring, a left-handed halfback who had come to the Bears directly from a Milwaukee high school, could throw a football farther than anyone I've ever known. He could heave a pigskin practically the distance of the playing field in the conventional way and could flip a pass from behind his back fifty-five yards. Hewitt, a tremendous competitor and an All-American from Michigan, went on in the pro ranks to establish himself as perhaps the greatest end who ever played football.

I toyed with the idea of hanging up my cleats for good after the 1932 campaign, but George Halas talked me into sticking around for a couple more seasons. My speed was gone by 1933—as attested by the fact that I made only one touchdown that year. No longer the first-string left halfback, I alternated at that position throughout the 1933 season with George Corbett, Gene Ronzani and Keith Molesworth. However, I did muster up enough strength to play a full sixty minutes in one game against the New York Giants when we nosed them out 14-10 on October 29th. I scored my one official touchdown on Thanksgiving Day, November 30th, when we beat the Chicago Cardinals 22-6—although three days later I had two more touchdowns which were called back for offsides when the Bears clinched the Western Division Title by beating Portsmouth 17-7. 1933 was the year in which the National Professional Football League was divided into the Western Division and Eastern Division with five teams each. On December 17th the Bears met the New York Giants, the winners of the Eastern Division Title, in Wrigley Field for the World Title and came out on top of a 23-21 score. Jack Manders, playing his first season with the Bears, accounted for 11 points in that championship clash with three field goals and two points after touchdown.

I received one of my greatest thrills in pro football

in that Bear-Giant championship battle. It happened in the last few seconds of play when, with the Bears ahead 23-21, the Giants seriously threatened to break up the game. Harry Newman, the New Yorkers' quarterback and former Michigan All-American, threw a desperate twenty-eight-yard pass to Halfback Dale Burnett who broke into the clear and out of reach of the Bear secondary. With Center Mel Hein running alongside of him, I was the only one Burnett had to elude to cross the goal line with the game-winning touchdown. I knew Burnett would lateral to Hein as soon as I tackled him, so I grabbed him high, wrapping my arms around his, thus preventing him from getting the ball away. As I pulled Burnett to the ground, the gun went off ending the game.

After winning their second consecutive World Title in 1933 with twelve wins, two losses and one tie, the Bears went on an eight-game Western exhibition tour and won all their games by a big margin. The Bears also won three exhibition games during the regular season. On the western trip we played the Los Angeles All-Stars in Wrigley Field, Los Angeles, before twenty-four thousand on January 14, 1934, and I contributed two touchdowns to our 26-7 victory. Both were made early in the first quarter. On the first one I cut over tackle, shook off two tacklers and ran seventy-four yards for the score. Homer Griffith of the University of Southern California, the All-Star quarterback who was to become the Chicago Cardinal's regular quarterback the following season, chased me the last thirty yards and failed in a last effort with a flying tackle at the goal line. Four minutes later, with the ball on our forty-five-yard line, "Bull" Doehring, the Bears' fabulous passer, tossed me a twenty-yard pass in the flat and I continued thirty-five more yards for the tally. I should have retired after that game, for I never had another day like that again. Most of the gains and touchdowns I made after my return to football in 1929 were on quick opening plays inside the ends. I was able, while I still had speed, to explode through the line for fairly consistent yardage, but, as I said earlier, couldn't do very much once I got into the open except run straight. My performance that day in Los Angeles was almost as if I were drawing my last dying breath as a football player.

The first Chicago *Tribune* sponsored All-Star football game was played at Soldier Field, Chicago, on Friday, August 31, 1934, with the champion Bears representing the pros against the college stars. The game ended in a 0-0 tie. I didn't get to play much because I was hurt in the first quarter when someone kneed me in the neck. Returning to the game in the final quarter, I managed to get off a pass good for a twenty-two-yard gain to Johnny Sisk, the Bears' right halfback, that enabled us to get down as far as the All-Stars' twenty-six-yard line, but our attack bogged down from there. Beattie Feathers of the University of Tennessee, who played left halfback for the College All-Stars, joined the Bear squad right after that game. In his first year with the Bears, the elusive, soft-spoken Feathers covered a record total of 1,004 yards from scrimmage, carrying the ball 117 times for an average of 8.5 yards per try. Feathers' ground-gaining record stood until 1949 when Steve Van Buren of the Philadelphia Eagles broke it with 1,146 yards.

In 1934 I hardly played at all on offense. I usually went in when the Bears were deep in their own territory. However, against the Cincinnati Reds on September 30, 1934, I scored one touchdown and got away for a seventeen-yard run as the Bears won the game 21-13. Three weeks later we played Cincinnati again and I scored another touchdown on a ten-yard pass from Doehring, then, later in the game, threw one myself to Quarterback Bernie Masterson for an eighteen-yard touchdown play as the Bears smothered the Reds 41-7. On November 4th I tallied once more as I took a pass from Quarterback George Corbett in the final period for a thirty-six-yard gain and a touchdown as we beat the New York Giants 27-7. That touchdown was the final one of my career and the 29th since my comeback in 1929. The week before that second game with Cincinnati, Saturday, October 13th, I had the thrill of being invited down to Champaign as the guest of honor of the University of Illinois on the occasion of their twenty-fifth Homecoming.

On Thanksgiving Day, November 29, 1934, the Bears beat the Detroit Lions 19-16 for their twelfth straight victory, and thereby sewed up the Western Division Title. Three days later the Bears beat the Lions again by a score of 10-7, and on December 9th met the Giants for the World Championship. New York took top honors in the Eastern Division in 1934

156

with eight wins and five losses. Many have considered the Bear team of that year—which, going into the championship game, had won thirteen games with no losses or ties—to be the greatest team in the history of college or professional football. In spite of the Bears' brilliant record for the season we lost the play-off game to New York 30-13. The Bears held a 10-3 advantage at half time, but the Giants came back to score four touchdowns and twenty-seven points in the last quarter, although they were unable to score more than nineteen points on us in eleven previous periods that season. New York accomplished this upset on a frozen field by wearing basketball shoes in the second half. Steve Owen, the Giants' coach, borrowed the shoes from nearby Manhattan College just before the game started. While the Bears slipped and skidded on their regulation football cleats as the field got more and more icy, the Giants' rubber-soled shoes enabled them to get a secure footing and they shoved the Bears around almost at will. From that day on, basketball shoes became regulation equipment for all pro-football teams for use in similar weather conditions.

Jack Manders, who was dubbed "Automatic Jack" for his incredible kicking ability, booted two field goals and one point after touchdown for the Bears in that play-off game. During the 1934 season Manders kicked ten field goals and established a record that was to stand until 1950, when Lou Groza of the Cleveland Browns topped it with thirteen. The hero of the Giants' victory was Ken Strong, a former New York University All-American, who piled up seventeen of his team's thirty points with two touchdowns, two conversions and one field goal.

On Sunday, January 27, 1935, the Bears defeated the New York Giants 21-0 in an exhibition clash before eighteen thousand in Hollywood's Gilmore Stadium—thus avenging the New Yorkers' win for the World's Championship five weeks earlier. Before going into that game I knew it was going to be my last appearance as an active player, as did my teammates and the Giant players. I played briefly in the first half, then went in again in the last quarter. The plan was to try and spring me loose for a touchdown at the first opportunity and, if lucky enough to score, I was going to lay the ball down in the end zone and walk right off the field. I almost made it, too. With the Bears in possession of the ball on their twenty-yard line, I took the pigskin and behind perfect blocking broke loose and got as far as mid-field, but my legs kept getting heavier and heavier as I ran. I just about reached the Giants' thirty-nine-yard line after a forty-one-yard run when Cecil Irvin, a 230-pound tackle, pulled me down from behind. Almost thirty-two years old, and more than eleven years since I played my first college game, it was obvious I had hit the end of the trail. The Bears were all pulling for me to make that last touchdown and were more disappointed than I when I failed to go the distance. Some of the Bear players were so mad at Irvin for catching up with me I was afraid they'd lynch him. As for myself, I didn't feel too badly. I had had more than my share of the breaks.

158

18

The Modern "T" Is Born

WHEN I PLAYED college football in 1923, 1924 and 1925, there were three basic offenses used by the coaches of the day. They were the single wing, which Zuppke used at Illinois, the double wing and the Notre Dame Box formations. The single wing was always played with an unbalanced line that generally shifted strong to the right. In this formation one halfback, who was called the wingback, stood about one yard back and a little bit outside of his own end on the strong side. The quarterback, who was the blocking back in the single wing, called the signals from about one yard behind his own right guard. The other halfback, called the tailback, took his position about four and a half yards directly behind the center and handled the ball on most plays, except on occasions when the fullback handled it on spinners and half spinners. The fullback's place in the single wing was about two yards to the right and slightly in front of the tailback. At Illinois I always played tailback. I also called signals from that position during the latter half of my senior year.

The double wing, like the single wing, had an unbalanced line. It differed from the latter formation only in that there were two wingbacks instead of one. This was accomplished by eliminating the fullback spot and moving the extra backfield man over to the identical position behind the end on the weak side as the one wingback in the single wing assumed on the strong side. The Notre Dame Box was about the same as the single wing—except that it was played with a balanced line with the fullback being moved more to the right to form a lopsided box. I wish to point out here that although the single- and double-wing formations were as I've described them, some coaches made slight alterations insofar as the spacing of the backs.

During the 1925 and 1929 seasons, my first two pro campaigns with the Chicago Bears, they were using what is known today as the old fashioned "T" formation. They were the only team to my knowledge in college and professional football who stuck to this formation even after the single wing became more popular. The old "T" used a balanced line with the quarterback stationed directly behind the center where he could take a hand-to-hand snap. The fullback stood about four yards directly behind the quarterback with the halfbacks close on each side of the fullback, directly behind their own guards. This compact formation used quick opening plays through guard and tackle for the most part, but wasn't very effective for wide plays.

The Bears continued with this type of "T" until 1930, when Ralph Jones took over the coaching reins from co-coaches George Halas and Edward "Dutch" Sternaman. Jones had been at Illinois from 1913 to

1920 as head basketball mentor and served as back-field coach under Bob Zuppke. Both Halas and Sternaman came in contact with Jones when they played at Illinois, and developed great confidence in him as a strategist and a leader.

When Jones became head coach of the Bears he did three things to the old "T" to transform it into what is now regarded as the modern "T." One, he moved the ends from one to two yards away from the tackles. Two, he widened the halfbacks so that they lined up straddling the outside leg of their own tackles. Three, he put a Man in Motion. These changes which were made to the old "T" resulted in opening up the defense by spreading them out and, consequently, opened up the entire game. The modern "T," like the old "T," is based on quick opening plays, but the big difference comes on pitchouts by the quarterback to the halfbacks or the fullback for wide end runs and also plenty of passing by the quarterback. Also, the single wing formation was based on power, where two men generally blocked one, while the "T" is based on deception, usually man for man blocking. In the "T" it isn't even necessary to knock the defensive man off his feet, because it strikes so lightning fast.

The Man in Motion portion of the modern "T" came about quite by accident on September 28, 1930, during a game between the Bears and the Green Bay Packers. Before we went into that contest, Jones instructed the halfback who was not slated to carry the ball to fake out to one side or the other depending upon which side the play went. After making one of those fakes myself in that game, Carl Brumbaugh, the Bears' quarterback, asked me when we came back in the huddle, "Is there anyone covering you on those wide fakes?" When I replied there wasn't, Brumbaugh ordered: "Then heads up this time, Red, 'cause I'm gonna throw you a lateral after you fake." There was no such play in our repertoire, but we often made up new plays in the huddle. We tried the play and I made a nice gain. On the next time out Brumbaugh and I talked about working it again. I suggested to him that inasmuch as football rules permit one back in motion laterally before the ball is snapped, it might be a good idea for me to start the fake out to the side a second or two before he took the hand-to-hand snap from center. Brumbaugh agreed to call the play that way and it worked so well we continued using it the rest of the game. This maneuver forced Green Bay to change their defense by pulling out one of their line backers to cover the Man in Motion, and thus gave them one less man to back up the line.

Although the Bears lost to the Packers 7 to 0 that day, Coach Ralph Jones, seeing the possibilities of the Man in Motion, immediately went to work on incorporating it as a regular part of his new "T" formation. When George Halas resumed his coaching chores of the Bears in 1933, he began the process of refining the modern "T" with the Man in Motion as an integral part of the new formation. He developed new plays, such as trap plays and delayed plays, invented counterplays, and unveiled a highly effective and intricate passing attack for the modern "T."

162

At the same time Halas took over the Bears' coaching reins again in 1933, Clark Shaughnessy, who gained considerable fame as head coach of Tulane and Loyola of the South, succeeded A. A. Stagg as head football coach of the University of Chicago. Shaughnessy became intrigued with the new football strategy employed by the Bears across town and, by 1936, began working with Halas on developing many new variations of the modern "T"—although he never attempted to use it while coaching at Chicago. In 1940, after football was abandoned on the Midway, Shaughnessy took over the head coaching spot at Stanford University and installed the modern "T" at the Pacific coast school exactly as the Bears played it. It was, to my knowledge, the first time the modern "T" with the Man in Motion was ever employed by a major college eleven. In 1939 the Stanford Indians were beaten seven times to wind up in last place in the Pacific Coast Conference, so Shaughnessy had nothing to lose and everything to gain by trying it. The experiment worked miracles as the Indians not only won the coast championship in 1940 with an undefeated season, but topped it off by defeating Nebraska 21-13 in the Rose Bowl on January 1, 1941, for the most spectacular season in the school's then fifty-year history. That same year the Chicago Bears beat the Washington Redskins by a whopping 73-0 score for the World Professional Football Championship. During the first ten years, from 1930 to 1940, that the Bears used the modern "T," they won three (1932, 1933, 1940) World Championships and two (1934, 1937) Western Division titles. With the phenomenal success of the Stan-

163

ford Indians and the Chicago Bears, almost every coach in college and pro ball was eager to jump on the modern "T" bandwagon. It was only a matter of a few years until the modern "T" became the most widely used football formation in the game.

I've heard some of the older coaches say they used the "T," as we know it today, almost forty years ago, but most football experts agree it was Jones who first put it in operation in 1930. If they did employ a "T" formation before 1930, it must have been the old fashioned "T." As far as I know, Ralph Jones originated the modern "T" and both George Halas and Clark Shaughnessy developed and perfected it. Today the modern "T" has taken on varied forms as many coaches employ their own particular versions of the formation. Two specific variations that come to mind are the split "T" and the wing "T," which are merely segments of the modern "T." The wing "T" is somewhat like the Notre Dame Box with the Man in Motion added to it, whereas the split "T" just widens the linemen and the halfbacks in the regular "T."

I believe that most players would rather play the "T" than any other formation, because it's less bruising and more fun. It can be compared to a chess or poker game where bluffing and faking the opposition is so important. The fans like it too, since it opens up the game more. And it's interesting to note that regardless of what has been accomplished to date, the surface has only been scratched on this new and progressive formation—the modern "T" is sure to become more highly developed every year.

164

19

The Years Following

AFTER I HUNG UP my cleats for good, following that game with the Giants in January, 1935, I remained with the Chicago Bears as an assistant coach for nearly three more seasons. After my first year in the coaching ranks, George Halas told me any time I wanted to take over as head coach of the Bears he would step out. I was highly flattered by Halas' offer, but didn't think I had enough experience for the job. Besides, I never had any ambition to be a head coach in either the professional or college ranks. A coach puts in four times as many hours as a player, is under constant strain to produce a winning team and must be prepared to take considerable abuse if he is unsuccessful in turning out a winner. It wasn't in my physical make-up to push myself that hard or work under such pressure.

In the fall of 1937, while I was still serving as an assistant to Halas, I got a call one day from the secretary of Jim Peterson, the president of Hinckley & Schmitt, a water and soft-drink company in Chicago. I was informed Mr. Peterson wanted to discuss a business matter with me. A luncheon date was set at the Union League Club. I never met the man before but, getting together for lunch, discovered he had graduated from Illinois the year before I entered and was one of my greatest rooters. He told me he saw just about every game I played in, both college and professional. When, during the course of conversation, Mr. Peterson asked me what my plans were for the future and I told him I had no desire to pursue coaching as a career, he said he could offer me a fine opportunity if I would be interested in going to work for him. Discussing his proposition in more detail a few days later I agreed to join his company as the sales-promotion manager. I tried to continue with my coaching chores with the Bears at the same time, but after about five weeks of that it got to be too much of a burden trying to hold down two jobs. In the middle of the 1937 football season I resigned my coaching position so I could devote full time to my new business connection. At this juncture I would like to mention that for most of the nine years I worked for Halas we never had a contract or a specified salary arrangement. He always gave me exactly what I thought I was worth. George Halas is not only one of the greatest figures in all football history as a strategist and leader, but one of the finest men I've ever known. His warm friendship through the years has meant a great deal to me.

I was associated with Jim Peterson's organization for five years, and during that time we became very good friends. One day, after I had been with him for about four years, he said to me, "Red, I shouldn't be saying this because I don't want to see you leave, but a guy like you ought to get into a business of your own.

166

That's the only way you'll ever make big money and be free to do all the things you want to do." That remark got me to thinking. Some time later a highly successful insurance man named Howard Potter, a friend of Peterson's, joined Jim and myself on a three-week vacation in Arizona. During the course of the trip Howard suggested I go into the insurance business. He said he was sure I could do well in that field and, best of all, it would afford me the opportunity to engage in other activities as well. The idea sounded appealing and Jim encouraged me to give the matter serious thought. I began studying for the brokers' examination when I got back to Chicago and, in September, 1942, left my job with Hinckley & Schmitt to become an insurance broker. I'm still in the insurance business today and it turned out to be the best thing that ever happened to me from a business standpoint.

Late one Friday night in the fall of 1940, I boarded an Omaha-bound United Air Lines plane in Chicago and, although I didn't realize it at the time, that flight turned out to be the greatest break of my life. I was headed for Lincoln, Nebraska, to do a radio interview show for an oil sponsor with coaches Biff Jones and Gwenn Henry of Nebraska and Kansas respectively, whose teams were scheduled to meet the next day. While working for Jim Peterson I kept myself busy with radio assignments and speaking engagements on week ends during the football season. Getting back to the flight, the stewardess on the plane was an attractive, friendly girl named Margaret Hazelberg. We got involved in conversation and she expressed a desire to see a Bear football game in Chicago, where she was headquartered. By promising to get her some tickets, I wangled her phone number. Within a few weeks we had our first date, and after that "Muggs" and I saw one another on and off for about a year—but she never did see the Bears play until some five years later. On October 13, 1941, we drove off by ourselves to Crown Point, Indiana, and were married. My only regret is that I didn't take that plane ride sooner. My wife has been a wonderful pal to me, a constant source of inspiration and unquestionably the finest "manager" a man could have.

After I became an insurance broker in the fall of 1942, I began to devote most of my spare time during the football season to radio and speaking engagements around the country. Although I had a busy schedule I filled whatever hours I had left working with youth groups and attending important football meetings such as the New York *Herald Tribune's* Coaches Clinic, where I appeared as one of the guest lecturers in 1946. By 1948 I was doing play-by-play accounts of football games every week on radio and television, as well as three other weekly radio and television shows. At the conclusion of the 1952 season I had done altogether sixty-one play-by-play games on network TV. As if this weren't enough to keep me busy, I was elected in November, 1950, to the Board of Trustees of the University of Illinois for a six-year term. I didn't seek the job nor did I have the slightest inkling that I was even being considered for the post. The first time I knew anything about it was when I read in the morning paper of August 12, 1950, that I was one of three Republicans nominated to run for the office in the November elections. The Republicans held their state convention the night before, while Harry Wismer and I were broadcasting the annual All-Star game between the College All-Stars and the Philadelphia Eagles in Soldier Field, Chicago. In spite of the heavy pressure of my other work, I felt it a great privilege to be able to serve my old school and one of the leading universities in the land.

In early April, 1951, the Associated Press, in conjunction with the National Football Hall of Fame, conducted a poll among one hundred leading sports writers from coast to coast to determine an All-Time, All-American football team. It was the first time anything like this had ever been done before on such a broad and representative scale, although the Chicago Bears organization picked an All-Time All-American team in 1946 on the basis of a poll they made of fans and sports writers. The Bears and AP polls honored me along with such greats as Bronko Nagurski, Willie Heston, Jim Thorpe, Don Hutson, Walter "Pudge" Heffelfinger, Benny Oosterbaan, Adolph "Germany" Schultz, Ernie Nevers, William "Fats" Henry, Jack Cannon, Sammy Baugh and others. I received a total of 704 points in the Associated Press poll for the largest point total of any of the other players named, making me an almost unanimous choice for one of the halfback positions on the All-Time All-American squad. It was a tribute of which I'm both proud and grateful.

Instead of slowing down as I got older, I quickened the pace. During the 1951 football season I literally burned the candle at both ends. Besides carrying on my regular insurance business, tending to my duties as a trustee of the University of Illinois and appearing as a speaker at about fifty football banquets, I attempted to carry what would normally be considered a full-time load of radio and television commitments. For example, on Mondays I transcribed a radio show, based on predictions of football games for the coming week, that was syndicated in about fifty cities. Tuesday and Thursday evenings I was on television. I did the Tuesday show with Luke Johnsos, a former teammate of mine and, for years, an assistant coach of the Chicago Bears. Called "The Chicago Bears Quarterback Club," it was a recap of the Bear game of the preceding Sunday. Luke and I started that TV show in 1948, and it has been on every fall since. On Friday nights I'd leave for some midwestern town where, on Saturdays, Bob Elson and I would broadcast an important Big Ten or Notre Dame game. Saturday nights found me on a plane bound for an Eastern city where I was to describe a National Professional Football game the next afternoon with Joe Hasel on one of the TV networks. And this was the schedule of the guy who thought he couldn't push himself or work too hard. It was a killing pace, but I didn't realize it because I so enjoyed what I was doing. After nearly three months of this, I began to show the effects of overwork. I was looking haggard and felt a fatigue I never knew before. My wife became concerned about my health and was

170

after me to slow down. I promised her I would take a good rest immediately after the season which, at that time, was only a few weeks away.

On Friday, December 14th, I went down to Kirksville, Missouri with Mark Cox, an executive of the Wilson Sporting Goods Company with which I was also associated in an advisory capacity. Mark's close friend was coach of the football team at the Northeast Missouri State Teachers College in Kirksville, and I promised to speak at the annual football banquet there. The week before I had been on a speaking tour of cities in Tennessee, Ohio, and South Dakota. I didn't feel right on the train to Kirksville. I lay down in our drawing room and didn't get up until we arrived in Kirksville where I rested in the hotel room during our entire stay except for the few hours I spent at the banquet. I began to feel worse when I left Kirksville and when I arrived in Chicago Saturday morning, I went straight home to bed. Muggs, who was a nurse before she became an airline stewardess, immediately took my temperature and it was 103. At first she thought I might have a virus infection, but when I seemed to get weaker as the day wore on, Muggs became alarmed and called Dr. Leonard S. Ceasar. The doctor, whose wife had been a stewardess with Muggs, came over and upon taking my blood pressure found it at a dangerously low 75. He summoned an ambulance at nine o'clock that night to take me to the hospital. I remember that as sick as I was, I was embarrassed when they carried me out of my apartment on a stretcher.

At the West Suburban Hospital in Oak Park, Illinois, the doctor's fears were confirmed when a cardiogram showed I had suffered a heart attack. I was shocked when I heard the news, for although I had incurred many injuries during my playing career, I was never seriously ill before. The doctor told me, "You've got a coronary, Red, but if you do everything I tell you, I'm sure you'll pull out of this and be all right again." For five weeks I remained glued to my hospital bed and my phone was cut off so I wouldn't be disturbed. My wife was my nurse. Staying with me day and night, she slept on a cot in my room at the hospital. In the afternoons Muggs would leave me just long enough to go down to my office to see that things were in order. While hospitalized I got stacks of cards and letters not only from friends, but from people I never even heard of. It helped a great deal to cheer me up.

For almost three months after I left the hospital I was confined to my home as a semi-invalid. At the end of this time I began to feel some of my strength coming back. My blood pressure went up to 127 and my cardiogram was normal again, or as normal as it could possibly be after a coronary. During my illness I went down from 210 pounds to 170 pounds—which was what I weighed when a sophomore in college. I now watch my diet closely, and intend to stay at that weight from here on in. I believe being overweight was an important factor in my getting sick.

Today, thanks to the splendid care given me by my doctor and my devoted wife, I am able to do almost everything I did before. The big difference is that what

I do now is done in moderation. During the 1952 football season I was on television twice weekly with "The Chicago Bears Quarterback Club" and my play-by-play reporting of all Chicago Cardinals and Chicago Bears home games. I also accepted a limited number of speaking dates. I go down to my office every day in the Insurance Exchange Building in Chicago, but leave by midafternoon so I can go home and rest. My siege in the hospital taught me how to relax and made me realize that one doesn't have to be active all the time to be happy. In a sense I consider myself lucky for having had that heart attack. I've been given a warning. Now that I'm cutting down on my activities and have learned the secret of relaxation, I hope to live on to a ripe old age.

20

In Retrospect

WHATEVER SUCCESS I may have achieved in sports can be credited to my father. I owe him everything for encouraging me to pursue my athletic activities and for insisting that I go to college. He wanted all the things for his sons that he didn't have for himself. Dad never interfered with anything I ever wanted to do and never gave advice unless I asked for it. And I seldom sought advice from him. He considered me a man when I was twenty-one years old and, as always, let me work out my own problems as best I could. "You're the fella who has to live with it," Dad would say. "If you believe in yourself you'll do what you think is right regardless of what I tell you." When things didn't work out for me as I had planned them, my father was all the more understanding and considerate. He would try consoling me with: "Don't let it get you down, Red. Like everyone else, you're gonna make a lot more mistakes in your lifetime." I was mighty lucky to have a father like that.

I got a great break at Illinois and nobody knows that better than I do. I ended up making most of the team's touchdowns and getting all the publicity, because Coach Bob Zuppke let me carry the ball 90 per cent of the time. In most of the games I carried the ball thirty to forty times. That I was given the ball often certainly wasn't enough—I had to be able to run well with it. But it was the ten other men on the field who enabled me to make the most of my running ability. Without them I could never have scored those touchdowns. They are the unsung heroes. One of the first things Zup taught me was that there are no one-man teams in football. "Football is a game of team-work," he'd say. "Let one man fall down and it can prevent a play from working. The player who carries the ball is no more important to a football team than any one of the other ten players. Because of the publicity given a ball carrier, the public may think of him as being more important, but everyone on the team including himself knows otherwise." I for one could never understand how a man who attains a measure of success in athletics or any other field can become conceited and overimpressed with himself. All that kind of a person has to do is make an honest evaluation of his case history and he'll be quick to realize that he couldn't possibly have accomplished what he did without the help of others.

I've often been asked by parents, do you think I should let my son play football? My answer has always been that a boy should never be forced into it, but if he displays an interest, then he should be encouraged. Also, parents should see to it that their boy plays with the proper equipment, gets some reliable instruction and coaching and plays with boys his own size. If a youngster plays football under these conditions

175

you'll never have to worry about him being able to take good care of himself. Let me emphasize here that a boy doesn't necessarily have to be a star. He can get a lot out of any competitive sport just by playing it. Participation in sports develops character and keeps a boy out of trouble. It teaches him discipline, fair play, how to withstand terrific pressure, and the meaning of working with other people. He also learns that hard work pays off, that one must be able to lose as well as win gracefully. I've long had the belief that as long as we have our young people engaging in competitive sports, our country will always remain in good hands.

In my opinion there are six factors that go into the making of a great athlete. First is ability. It isn't necessary for a boy to have an excessive amount of ability, but he must be able to do certain things which are required for the particular sport in which he participates. Second, he must begin working on developing his body and his ability when he is ten, eleven or twelve years old. That's the time to start forming good habits and correcting bad ones. A boy can avoid a lot of pitfalls later if he starts out early enough. Third, a boy must have intelligence. I don't believe there ever was a great athlete who was slow-witted, because it is impossible to survive in athletics without having to do a considerable amount of thinking for yourself. Fourth is courage; and courage takes various forms such as running head-on into a 250-pound lineman, or stepping up to the free-throw line in a close basketball game. Fifth, a boy must have a love for athletics. It's not all fun to be a great athlete. It means lots of hard work and giving up many of the pleasures of life. In back of all the glory an athlete receives the day of the big game are countless hours devoted to training and practicing. Sixth and last, but by no means least, is determination. If a boy is to succeed he must be determined to do so. Success in athletics like anything else won't come to him merely because he wants it, has ability or started out at a young age. A boy has to give it all he's got at all times.

While I'm at it I might as well write what I think it is that makes a great football coach. There are many hundreds of young football coaches in the country today who may have as much technical knowledge of football as a Bob Zuppke, a Pop Warner, an Amos Alonzo Stagg, a Knute Rockne, a Fielding Yost or a George Halas. But they lack that certain something that the Zuppkes and the Rocknes had in their personalities that made them the coaching geniuses they were. Besides being outstanding strategists and untiring workers, those coaching immortals had the rare gift of being able to get the most out of their players. They knew exactly how to handle their men. It was instinctive with them. That was their greatness. To have played under any of their banners was a privilege indeed.

In conclusion, I wish to say that I shall be forever grateful to the great game of football for all that it has done for me. Through football I've been able to meet and get to know many thousands of wonderful people. Football has brought me not only stimulating acquaintances, but enduring friendships as well. Football has enabled me to do and see most of the things I wanted in life and made it possible to earn a good living through the years. Thanks to football, I feel I've had a truly exciting and interesting life. For the benefit of the younger set who may have read this book, may I again recall for the purpose of bringing out a moral, that when I was a kid the only thing I thought about was athletics. It was my whole life and I put everything I had into it. The future took care of itself. When the breaks came I was ready for them. Any boy can realize his dreams if he's willing to work and make sacrifices along the way.

For the Record

Red Grange's record at the University of Illinois

1923 Season:		M.P.	T.	Yds. by Running	P.	Yds. by Passing
Illinois 24, Nebraska	7	39	3	202		
Illinois 21, Butler	7	28	2	142		
Illinois 9, Iowa	6	60	1	174		
Illinois 29, Northwestern	0	19	3	247		
Illinois 7, Chicago	0	59	1	173		
Illinois 10, Wisconsin	0	30	1	139		
*Illinois 27, Mississippi A&M	0					
Illinois 9, Ohio State	0	60	1	183		
Totals		295	12	1,260		
1924 Season:						
Illinois 9, Nebraska	6	60	0	116	6	127
Illinois 40, Butler	0	16	2	104	2	42
Illinois 39, Michigan	14	41	5	402	6	78
*Illinois 45, De Pauw	0					
Illinois 36, Iowa	0	45	2	186	3	86
Illinois 21, Chicago	21	60	3	300	7	150
Illinois 7, Minnesota	20	44	1	56	3	41
*Illinois 7, Ohio State	0					
Totals		266	13	1,164	27	524
1925 Season:						
Illinois 0, Nebraska	14	51	0	57	1	18
Illinois 16, Butler	13	41	2	196	2	22
Illinois 10, Iowa	12	60	1	233	2	24
Illinois 0, Michigan	3	60	0	147	0	0
Illinois 24, Pennsylvania	2	57	3	363	1	13
Illinois 13, Chicago	6	60	0	64	0	0
**Illinois 21, Wabash	0	5	0	0	0	0
Illinois 14, Ohio State	9	48	0	153	9	42
Totals		382	6	1,213	15	119

*Did not play.
**Made only an appearance. Did not carry the ball.

Grand total at the University of Illinois: 938 minutes played; 31 touchdowns; 3,637 yards gained by running; 42 passes completed; 643 yards gained by passing; 4,280 yards gained by running and passing.

Scoring record at Wheaton High School, 1919 through 1921:
  75 touchdowns; 82 conversions. Total: 532 points.

Scoring record at the University of Illinois, 1923 through 1925:
  31 touchdowns. Total: 186 Points.

*Scoring record with the Chicago Bears–New York Yankees, 1925 through 1934:
  56 touchdowns; 4 conversions. Total: 340 Points.

Grand total in high-school, college, and professional football:
  162 touchdowns; 86 conversions. Total: 1,058 Points.

*Inactive during 1928 Season.

_____

Red Grange's physical measurements
during his senior year in college

Neck .... 15.6 inches
Wrist .... 8 inches
Reach .... 74 inches
Arm Length................. 30 inches
Biceps .... 14¾ inches
Chest, normal.............. 38 inches
Chest, expanded .... 44 inches
Waist .... 35 inches
Thigh .... 23½ inches
Calf .... 16 inches
Ankle .... 10 inches
Height .... 5 ft. 11 inches
Weight .... 175 pounds
Age: 22

Afterword

In 1954, Red Grange and his wife, Margaret, whom he affectionately called "Muggs," left Chicago and moved to Florida. They had been thinking about making the move for a long time. Both had traveled extensively and chose the area for their retirement because of its temperate year-round climate.

The Granges first lived in Miami, then after a few years settled in a beautiful new residential community in central Florida called Indian Lakes Estates. There they built their dream house, which Red designed himself. It was a comfortable, moderately sized ranch house with an indoor swimming pool, a lush garden, and a lagoon situated at the edge of their backyard. They kept a small cabin cruiser tied up at their pier and often went for leisurely spins around the nearby lake. Red also enjoyed tending his garden, trimming bushes and trees, and doing odd jobs around the house.

Wildlife abounded near the Grange home. Red loved to feed the quail, rabbits, and Sandhill cranes that came up to the front door looking for food. He once tried to make a pet of a baby alligator that lived in the lagoon and kept popping up around the pier. He fed it regularly by hand but wisely gave up the practice after a few months when the creature began to show signs of aggression.

From the time Red moved to Florida until his full retirement in 1969 he continued to work part-time during the football season as a public relations representative for a national beverage company and a sportscaster for college and professional football games. When he finally left the broadcast booth after a twenty-nine-year career, Red estimated he had covered about 480 games on both radio and television (included in that number were thirty-two bowl games). To the best of my knowledge he was the first prominent athlete to be hired as a full-fledged sportscaster. His experience, expertise, and insight as a player impressed broadcast executives and enabled him to bring an added dimension to play-by-play and color reporting—and thus open up new opportunities for other athletes who had once excelled in their sport.

Red was sixty-six years old when he cashed in his chips and withdrew from all business commitments. He was in a position to retire without any financial worries, something it had taken a long time and an extraordinary amount of grit and determination to achieve. During his heyday as a football player he had invested heavily in a new football franchise and in the stock market. When the team faltered financially and the market crashed in 1929, Red was wiped out, but he worked feverishly for the next forty years to recoup his losses. Red had experienced hard times as a child and as a young man, and he resolved never to be in that position again.

In 1963, six years before his retirement, Red Grange was inducted into the Professional Football Hall of Fame as a charter member. Jim Thorpe, Bronko Nagurski, George Halas, Cal Hubbard, George Marshall, Earl "Curly" Lambeau, Johnny "Blood" McNally, Bert Bell, Joe Carr, Ernie Nevers, and Earl "Dutch" Clark were the other inductees in that initial ceremony. It was one of the most memorable and significant tributes Red was to receive during his lifetime, matched only by an event that took place eleven years later.

On October 19, 1974, Red returned to the University of Illinois for "Red Grange Day." More than 55,000 students, faculty, alumni, and Illini football fans turned out to commemorate the fiftieth anniversary of the dedication of Memorial Stadium and to celebrate Red's historic 1924 performance against the University of Michigan. The Wolverines once again provided the opposition, but instead of a 39-14 Illinois rout, the teams played to a 21-21 tie. The outcome mattered little to most of those in attendance. What they had come to see was the return of "The Galloping Ghost" to hallowed ground.

Red did not disappoint the crowd. Just before game time he acknowledged a standing ovation with a big smile and hands held high as he walked from the horseshoe entrance at the south end of the field to his eastside box on the fifty-yard line. When formally introduced at the special halftime ceremonies, his voice was filled with emotion as he thanked everyone for remembering him after so many years. During the game he signed autographs, shook every outstretched hand, posed for pictures, and responded to almost every request from the horde of media people. His presence

183

that day was living testimony to a glorious period in the university's athletic history.

Four years later, Red made his final trip to the Midwest, this time for a visit to his hometown of Wheaton, Illinois. He went for the dedication of the DuPage Heritage Gallery and the Red Grange Archives, which houses a vast collection of Grange memorabilia. James R. Thompson, then governor of Illinois and the main speaker, said during the course of his remarks: "As individuals, as residents of a community, as citizens of our Republic and as members of the human race we need to have heroes . . . heroes as exemplars of those rare men and women whose spirit transcends any category, a Red Grange."

In January 1980, NBC-TV devoted an entire "Tomorrow" show to an interview with Red. Host Tom Snyder did his portion of the telecast from a studio in New York, while Red appeared via satellite from his home in Florida. It was a very informal visit with Snyder asking various questions about Red's football career and his life as a "retired gentleman." As usual, Red left it up to the interviewer to recall his legendary feats on the gridiron while he concentrated on telling humorous anecdotes about players, coaches, and game officials. At one point, Snyder asked a question that he hoped would generate a historic response: "How did you happen to get your famous number 77"? With a twinkle in his eye Red replied, "When I was a freshman, I stood in the line where they were passing out uniforms. The guy in front of me was handed the uniform with number 76 on it and the guy behind he got number 78." This was pretty much the tone of the entire interview. Snyder and the program's viewers loved it.

In February 1981, Red left the sunshine of Florida and braved the cold and snow of New Haven, Connecticut, to attend an elegant black-tie dinner at Yale University Commons. It was the Fourteenth Annual Awards Dinner of the Walter Camp Foundation. Six different awards were given out that night, and Red was there to receive the most prestigious one of all: the Walter Camp Distinguished American Award. The accompanying citation read: "Whenever and wherever football fans gather, the shadow of The Galloping Ghost is cast across the field. Throughout his career and thereafter, Harold "Red" Grange came to represent the best in American sportsmanship. He is a leader, an innovator and pioneer who was so outstanding in the development of his talents, his accomplishments must not pass without being recognized by the Walter Camp Foundation." Red responded to this great honor with his typical self-effacing humor. "I'm thrilled to be here," he said. "I heard about Yale when I was a poor kid growing up in Wheaton, and the closest I ever thought I'd get to this place was to poke my nose in the back door and take a quick look around."

When Red turned eighty on June 13, 1983, just about every small-town and big-city newspaper in the land noted the occasion with feature stories recalling his contributions to the game of football and to sports in general. In Forksville, Pennsylvania, where he was born, the residents of that still small community gathered for a birthday party in his honor. At this point in his life

185

he had ruled out all travel, but he willingly agreed to speak to the devoted townsfolk via a special speaker-phone hookup.

For Red, the winter of his life was indeed sweet. His health was excellent at the time of his retirement and remained so until about three years before his passing. He thoroughly enjoyed being free of responsibilities, and when asked what he did with his time he would smile broadly and answer, "I do nothing." When the infirmities of age set in, he accepted them stoically and without complaint. After his heart attack at age forty-eight, he did not expect to reach his number "77" and considered every year past forty-eight a bonus. Confined to a nursing home in the last few months of his life, he died peacefully on January 28, 1991, at the age of eighty-seven, just nine months before he and his beloved Muggs were to celebrate their fiftieth wedding anniversary.

Red Grange surely enjoyed the public acclaim he received during his lifetime. He would not have been human if he hadn't. But I have always believed that deep down he never fully understood why everyone made such a fuss over him. Such was the depth of his humility. The world of sports may never see the likes of him again.

Ira Morton
Phoenix, Arizona